LADDER OF ABHYASA
Practical guide to meditation

Books and Booklets By J.P. Vaswani

In English:

The Seven Commandments of the Bhagvad
    Gita
Kill Fear Before Fear Kills You
Swallow Irritation Before Irritation Swallows
    You
Its All A Matter of Attitude
You Can Make A Difference
101 Stories For You and Me
108 Pearls of Practical Wisdom
108 Simple Prayers of a Simple Man
108 Thoughts On Success
114 Thoughts on Love
A Child of God
A Day with Dadaji
A Mystic of Modern India
Begin the Day with God
Beloved Dadaji
Conversations with Dadaji
Dada Answers
Daily Appointment With God
Daily Inspiration
Doors of Heaven
Education: What India Needs
Feast of Love
Five Fragrant Flowers
From Darkness Into Light
From Hell to Heaven
Glimpses
Glimpses Into Great Lives
God In Quest of Man
Hinduism
How to Have Real Fun Out of Life and
    other Talks
How to Make Your Life A Love Story
How to Overcome Temptations
How to Overcome Tensions
I Have Need of You
I Luv U, God!
Invest in the Child
Joy Peace Pills
Laugh Your Way to Health
Life After Death
Life is A Love Story
Love and Laugh!
Nestle Now
Notes from the Master's Lute
Pictures and Parables
Positive Power of Thanksgiving

Prayers of a Pilgrim
Prophets and Patriots
Sadhu Vaswani: His Life and Teachings
Little Lamps
Secrets of Health and Happiness
Shanti Speaks
Snacks for the Soul
More Snacks for the Soul
Stories for Meditation
Stories for You and Me
Teach Me to Pray
Tear-Drops (poems)
Temple Flowers
Ten Commandents of A Successful Marriage
The Holy Man of Hyderabad
The Kingdom of Krishna
A Little Book of Life
A Little Book of Wisdom
The Little Book of Prayer
The Little Book of Service
The Little Book of Success
The Little Book of Yoga
The Little Book of Freedom From Stress
The Magic of Forgiveness
The Simple Way
The Story of a Simple Man
The Way of Abhyasa (How to Meditate)
Ticket to Heaven
Twinkle, Twinkle Tiny Star
What you would like to know about Karma
Whispers
Why Do Good People Suffer?
You Are Not Alone!
You Can Be a Smile Millionaire
Destination Happiness
Ladder of Abhyasa

In Hindi:

Ishwar Tujhe Pranaam
Prarthna Ki Shakti
Alwar Santon Ki Mahaan Gaathaayein
Atmik Jalpaan
Atmik Poshan
Bhale Logon Ke Saath Bura Kyon
Chitra Darshan
Dainik Prerna
Krodh Ko Jalayen, Swayam Ko Nahi
Mahan Purush Jeevan Darshan
Santon Ki Lila
Mrityun Hai Dwaar Phir Kya

Published by
Sterling Publishers Private Limited

LADDER OF ABHYASA
Practical guide to meditation

J. P. Vaswani

Sterling Paperbacks

STERLING PAPERBACKS
An imprint of
Sterling Publishers (P) Ltd.
A-59, Okhla Industrial Area, Phase-II,
New Delhi-110020.
Tel: 26387070, 26386209; Fax: 91-11-26383788
E-mail: sterlingpublishers@airtelbroadband.in
ghai@nde.vsnl.net.in
www.sterlingpublishers.com

Ladder of Abhyasa

© 2007, J. P. Vaswani

ISBN 978 81 207 3491 3

Printed and Published by Sterling Publishers Pvt. Ltd.,
New Delhi-110 020.

Contents

1. The Journey Within   2
2. The World Within   6
3. Impediments On The Journey Within   10
4. Help Is At Hand!   16
5. Practise Silence, Every Day   20
6. The Treasure Of Tears   26
7. Self-Discipline Is The Key!   32
8. What Is Meditation?   53
9. Meditation And The Life Of Work   65
10. Which Is The Right Way To Meditate?   69
11. Why Should You Meditate?   73
12. Preparing To Meditate: Where And When?   76
13. Quietening The Mind   87
14. How Do I Proceed?   91
15. The Power Of Concentration   96
16. How Long Should You Meditate?   100
17. The Value Of *Mantra*   103
18. The Power Of the Form   110
19. Meditation For All   117
20. Experiences During Meditation   120
21. Relax! Relax! Relax!   123

22. A Simple Exercise   127
23. Health And Healing Through Meditation   131
24. *Sutras*   136
25. Guided Meditations   148
26. Meditation Exercises For You   167
27. FAQs On The Ladder Of Abhyasa   183

Meditation is the gateway, through which you arrive to the world of freedom.

Remez Sasson

Pilgrimages there are many. But if I have not entered upon the interior pilgrimage, I have wasted the golden opportunity of the human birth.

J. P. V.

The Journey Within

Which is the most exciting journey you have ever undertaken?

Some of you would recall memorable trips to a hill-station, a seaside resort or a historic location.

Some of you, who have traveled more widely, would think of adventurous journeys to exotic, far-off places – may be the Great Barrier Reef, may be the African Serengeti, may be Hawaii or Honolulu, Scandinavia, Corsica, Bali or Tibet...

I would like to talk to you about a far more exciting journey that all of us can undertake at will; we don't need a lot of money – so all of us can try it! Passports, visas, flight and train bookings are not needed – all we need is the desire, the determination, the focus to get to our destination!

I can hear some of you asking, "We're ready! Just tell us where we are going – and it had better be really exciting!"

Again, some of you might say, "I am not really interested in getting to one of those popular destinations. I am fed up of crowds and queues!"

Some of you may even add, with a dose of world-weariness, "Look, there are hardly any places I have *not* been to – so this had better be good!"

My promise to all of you is that your destination is going to be a totally new, unexplored territory with the most exciting possibilities. I assure you that you will find it exciting and fascinating – for I am going to take you on a journey WITHIN.

Have you heard of Jules Verne? He wrote wonderful novels in the nineteenth century, about thrilling voyages and trips: *Around the World in Eighty Days, Twenty Thousand Leagues Under the Sea* and *Journey to the Centre of the Earth*. Even today, these books are hailed for their vision and insight into the future.

How about a journey to the Centre of your Consciousness? Have you ever considered the possibility of undertaking such a journey inward?

Perhaps at this stage, some of you will feel a distinct sense of disappointment: "Inward? *Within* me? But today, people are booking passages on space flights to explore the Universe..."

True, man has progressed far in the study of the world outside; but what about the unexplored realms of the world inside?

Friends in Chennai tell me that every day, hundreds and hundreds of villagers from the interiors of peninsular India arrive in the city for sightseeing. The tourist buses take them straight to Chennai's famous Marina beach and they get their first glimpse of the sea— and they are enthralled! Eyes round with astonishment, mouths wide open in sheer amazement, they stare at the vast expanse of blue waters before them—for they have never seen anything like this before!

"Oh really," you may protest. "Wherever you are in the world, you only have to travel a few hundred miles and you will be in sight of a sea or an ocean. So what's the big deal?"

True, even in landlocked interior Russia or central Europe, if one travelled for a couple of days one could get to the seaside. But do you know there are people who simply have not made that effort for one reason or another?

An American writer speaks about a native Indian tribe living barely thirty miles away from the Western Coast of the U.S. Some of them did not know of the existence of the Pacific Ocean, when explorers first discovered their settlement in the early nineteenth century.

Why hadn't these people walked twenty-odd miles to see one of the most breathtaking sights of North America?

There was a rational explanation for that, too. A high ridge separated them from the coast. The valley they lived in was thus 'cut off' from the world outside, and they found no reason to look beyond the mountain to explore what lay ahead.

The Chinese proverb tells us that even the longest of journeys must begin with the first step. So the starting point is obvious: we have to take the first step!

What lies behind us and what lies before us are tiny matters compared to what lies within us.

Ralph Waldo Emerson

Superficiality characterises everything we do. We judge people by the clothes they wear and the cars they drive. We occupy our minds with what we would like to eat, what we would like to buy and what we could do to impress friends and neighbours. We have no time to think of the world within!

J. P. V.

The World Within

Psychologists tell us that there are three 'states' in which human beings exist: the waking state, the sleeping state and the dreaming state.

Perhaps, psychology stops a little short; for our ancient sages spoke of a fourth state of intense concentration beyond these three – a state of which most of us are unaware.

An American friend once said to me, "Here in the Western World, we have three states of awareness which are different from yours: we are asleep, we are awake or we are watching TV!"

Perhaps Westerners are not the only ones; many of us are in complete ignorance of this whole dimension of awareness that exists within us.

The question is, how many of us are willing to explore this kingdom within?

We are content to live our lives on the surface. Superficiality characterises everything we do. We judge other people by the clothes they wear and the cars they drive. We occupy our minds with what we would like to eat, what we would like to buy and what we could do to impress friends and neighbours. At the farthest, we save for the future and we make sure that there is enough money for us to spend in old age.

We have no time to think of the world within!

"Alright, alright," you may exclaim impatiently. "Can you please tell us what we are likely to find in this world within, about which you speak so eloquently?"

I'll be happy to tell you what you will find within you: *not* material treasures; *not* the wealth of this world – but untapped, undreamt of resources of wisdom, peace, joy, spiritual strength, creativity and healing power!

In our constant state of superficial existence, we continue to ignore the world within. In our persistent chase after shadow-shapes and worldly wealth, we lose sight of our inner consciousness. We emphasise speech, action and outward show; we forget that there is a far more valuable aspect to life called reflection, contemplation, introspection. Men and women of speech and action, there are very many; alas, men and women of reflection and contemplation, there are very few.

A leading practitioner of meditation in the U.S. once pointed out that several cultures and religions simply do not teach people to focus on the world within them; their emphasis is often on words, rites and rituals; on a Form or a Being or Spirit *outside*; thus the innermost Spirit remains out of reach of most people.

The Indian tradition on the other hand, has always placed great value on meditation, reflection and contemplation – on the state of inner silence and inner stillness. For, it is in this state that we will find tranquility, serenity, self-knowledge and true awareness. In this state, too, we will experience true freedom – freedom from the fears, desires, tensions, insecurities and complexes that haunt us in the waking state. In this state of inner consciousness, we will also

7

discover our own Divinity – that we are not the bodies we wear, we are not the insignificant, pathetic, frail creatures that we take ourselves to be; we will discover that we are the immortal *atman*, the eternal, infinite spirit that is *Sat-chit-ananda* – pure, true, eternal Bliss!

Man is most uniquely human when he turns obstacles into opportunities.

Eric Hoffer

We need to protect ourselves against the three pronged attack of *maya* – the desire for pleasure, wealth and power.

Therefore, we must continually pray for God's grace!

J. P. V.

Impediments On The Journey Within

A friend of mine, who is a teacher, said to me the other day, "Dada, my students are the most imaginative and inventive people I have ever met."

"Is that so?" I said with interest. "Are they like those brilliant young innovators and inventors who think differently and find brilliant new solutions to problems? Do tell me what your students have been up to!"

"Oh no, Dada, I did not mean that, not at all," he laughed. "My students give me the most amazing, inventive, unheard of excuses for *not* doing their work, *not* submitting their assignments on time, and *not* doing well in the examinations."

He went on to say that excuses like, "I was unwell," or "My great grandfather is dead" had all become outdated now. "There was a power failure,"; "My computer broke down,"; "My floppy is not opening,"; "I have an interview for a part time job this week," are some of the new excuses he gets now. Students also add that they are attending CAT, SAT, GMAT or GRE classes – or sitting for these exams, as they are famously known.

We may laugh at these young people; but when it comes to meditation or even the practice of silence, we are no different from these 'innovators' and 'inventors' of excuses.

The great Maharishi Patanjali himself warns us about the *antarayas* or obstacles which we encounter on the path of *yoga* – and these also apply to meditation, the journey within:

1. Illness is obviously an impediment; when you are in a disturbed frame of mind or physically unfit, you cannot meditate successfully. Patanjali warns us that meditation should not be taught to those who lack emotional balance and maturity. Negative states of mind like arrogance, anger, hostility and hatred are also not conducive to meditation. We must also realize that physical ailments affect both body and mind. It is better that we do not begin to practise meditation in such conditions.

2. Lethargy or *tamas* is a state induced by overeating, over indulgence, or occasionally even by extreme weather conditions. We feel low and depleted; we feel 'heavy' in body and mind; we find that we cannot do anything useful or constructive. Our moods have a definite bearing on our minds, and it is better that we avoid such conditions.

3. Doubt or *samasya* is a negative feeling which fills us with uncertainty and pessimism. This can also undermine our effort to meditate.

4. Haste, leading to rashness and impatience is not suited for the practice of meditation. We will only slip instead of making progress on the path.

5. Fatigue or exhaustion, known as *alasya* is also a debilitating condition. Our confidence is undermined, our energy levels are low. We need to be rejuvenated, remotivated before we can embark on meditation.

11

6. Distraction or *avirati* disturbs our powers of concentration. It diverts our mind from the chosen path and may even lead us to needless temptations. When we are led in the wrong direction, we lose the power of concentration.
7. Arrogance and pride are serious hurdles on the path of meditation. Those who are satisfied, complacent and vain, think that they know everything; they are in a state of *avidya* or ignorance and they cannot focus on meditation.
8. There is also the sense of an *inability to proceed*. We are discouraged and disheartened by what we perceive as our failure to progress. We may have even taken the first few steps, but feel that we are not getting anywhere. We despair of ever achieving our goal. This is hardly a helpful attitude.
9. Loss of confidence is the consequence of our own inability to proceed. We fall back and lose the motivation to pursue our goal.

These obstacles, as I have said, are mentioned by Patanjali. But they are not all. Living in a modern world of allurements and entanglements, we face many more such obstacles or "attitude problems".

1. "I have no time!" we proclaim loudly. We have time for TV, time to gossip, time to fool around, time to 'browse the web' mindlessly- but no time for ourselves, no time to discover the hidden treasures within us.
2. "I don't live alone!" we protest. Friends, family, colleagues, neighbours, customers and business contacts are all entitled to their claims upon us. We respect their demands, but we ignore our own deeper needs.

3. "I have other needs!" we insist. We are anxious to make more money; we are eager to become more powerful; we seek fame and popularity; and we decide that meditation and the inner world can wait.

There are other factors too, that hinder our progress:
1. Desire for sense-gratification:

Sri Ramakrishna spoke of 'Kamini', the personification of sense-indulgence, as one whom we must guard against.

There is a fable about a bee which found a pot of honey left near the hive. The bee thought to itself, "Why should I labour all day, flying from flower to flower, gathering honey so painstakingly? Here is a store of honey—I can reach it easily, and it's all mine!"

So the bee went into the pot, determined to revel in the sweet treasure. But it found its wings and feet clogged—it could not drag itself out of the sticky mess! It died—and was buried in its own pleasure!

We are told that the devil once called for a meeting of all its associates. It was a stock-taking session to determine which of them could wreck the greatest havoc on mankind.

Anger, jealousy, greed and envy were present, among others. Each one boasted of his numerous victims. Soon, a heated argument ensued; who, among them, could cause the most damage?

Impurity won, hands down. Conferring the dubious distinction upon him, the devil remarked; "He is the one with the sharpest sword, the deadliest weapon. All he has to do is to sow a single thought of impurity in the mind—and that will take care of the rest."

When lust, desire, greed and craving dominate our minds, how can we embark upon any spiritual practice?

2. Desire for wealth, for material possessions:

We all know the story of King Midas. He thought he had all that he would ever wish for, when everything that he touched, turned to gold. He learned the hard way that gold could not appease his hunger!

3. Desire for power, position and fame:

Alas! Some of us stoop very low to gain power, position and authority. After all, why are graft, corruption and bribery so rampant in the world today? Why are flattery, falsehood and hypocrisy so prevalent among the mighty and the powerful? Such practices only point to the lowest elements in human nature. They taint our minds and hearts and impede our spiritual progress – the only progress that matters.

Let us but ask ourselves: what is it that we seek through wealth, power and sense-indulgence? Where will they lead us eventually? Of what avail is earthly greatness and worldly wealth when we know that the call can come anytime for us – and we shall be reduced to an urn full of dust and ashes!

Alas, our minds are scattered. They are dispersed, tainted with desires, they look downwards. We need to purify our minds: we need to raise the level of our consciousness. We must learn to look upward, onward. We need to protect ourselves against the three pronged attack of *maya* – the desire for pleasure, wealth and power.

How may we overcome these obstacles?

14

Each difficulty is an opportunity for progress. To complain is a sign of weakness and insincerity.

Sri Aurobindo

A Guru inspires us by his living example. He sees the potential in us that we ourselves are not aware of. He provides tremendous power of incentive and inspiration and cures us of crippling negative emotions.

As the seeker proceeds on the path, he must never forget that he is always under the umbrella of his Guru.

The Guru is the great protector.

J. P. V.

Help Is At Hand!

Students of yoga, aspirants who wish to learn meditation—wherever they may be—have this in common: they value inner peace, harmony and serenity. They are eager and determined to probe the depths of the true Self, and they have made a serious commitment to the way of *abhyasa*. And in order to succeed on the chosen path, they make every effort to conquer both outer distractions and inner impediments.

In the Gita, we are given a memorable picture of a tortoise. Once the tortoise draws in its limbs, you will not be able to draw them out, even if you cut the creature into four pieces! This is the kind of determination you too, will need, if you wish to tread the way of *abhyasa*.

How may we achieve this?

1. We must pray, again and again. Pray with full consciousness. Pray to the Lord with utmost faith. Pray in the awareness that you are God's child and He will do only what is best for you.

   Pray to Him honestly, in simplicity, with longing and sincerity. Words and images are not what matters in prayer: feelings are far more important. Therefore, pray with deep feelings.

2. Seek the guidance of a Guru, a spiritual mentor. Spending time in the presence of an evolved soul is

16

the most powerful source of strength and inner wisdom. A Guru inspires us by his living example. He sees the potential in us that we ourselves are not aware of. Above all he encourages us to believe that we are also capable of achieving what he has! He provides tremendous powers of incentive and inspiration. He cures us of crippling negative emotions.

3. Start with *Karma Yoga* – before you set out in search of the inner self. Even those of us who feel diffident to tread the way of *abhyasa* can prepare themselves effectively by undertaking acts of selfless service. When we go out of our way to help and serve others, without claiming credit, without any thought of reward, we automatically purify our *antah karna* or inner instrument.

4. Cultivate self-discipline. The Gita teaches us that *tamas* is overcome by *rajas* – the principle of action, energy and dynamism. When we cultivate discipline of the mind, it will automatically lead us to *sattva* – light and harmony. With this enlightenment, our spiritual progress can be really speedy.

5. Eat right. *Sattvic* food, food of non-violence, will provide us with the right energy and the right frame of mind to pursue the path of *abhyasa*.

6. Offer all that you are, all that you have, all that you do, to the Lord, in a spirit of *arpanam*.

Sri Krishna tells us in the Gita: "Whatever you eat, whatever you give in charity, whatever austerity you practise, whatever you do, O Arjuna, do it as an offering unto Me."

This is the best antidote to conquer the ego and negate pride and arrogance. Whatever you do, offer

17

it to God. Whatever you achieve, it is His grace, His doing. Therefore, say to Him: I am not the doer. I am but a broken instrument. If there are any shortcomings, any mistakes that I make, they are mine. But all glory belongs to Thee!

Stop saying *I did it. This is mine. I worked hard for it. I earned it.* Instead say: *Everything is Thine. The energy is Thine. Nothing belongs to me. I am Thine.*

7. Cultivate the virtue of patience. Remember, haste makes waste. There are no short cuts, no instant solutions and no quick fixes on the path of *abhyasa*.

8. Remember, practice makes perfect. Ask any great athlete, any great singer, any great actor – and they will tell you that hours of effort and hard work have gone into their achievements. The inner light we seek to find is one of the greatest goals a human being can aim for. Therefore, give it all you have got!

Make meditation a daily practice, and it will soon turn into a habit.

Remez Sasson

We live in a world of deafening noises. Particles of noise cling to our souls: they need to be washed in the waters of silence. Silence cleanses. Silence heals. Silence strengthens and Silence reveals!

Truly, Silence is the Mother of God! It is in the depths of Silence that man beholds God, face to face.

J. P. V.

Practise Silence, Every Day

We live in a world of deafening noises. Particles of noise cling to our souls: they need to be washed in the waters of silence. Silence cleanses. Silence heals. Silence strengthens.

And silence reveals. Silence will bring you face to face with yourself.

Who are you? Other people have told you many things about yourself — some complimentary, some otherwise. But all that is not really you. You must now try to find who you are. This is the biggest challenge of life. You must discover yourself. It is not easy to do so— but it can be done!

Mullah Nasruddin was out in the street searching for something.

"What are you looking for?" they asked him.

"I have lost my keys," he answered.

"Where did you lose them?" he was asked.

And he said, "I lost them in the house."

"Then how is it that you are looking for them here?"

And the Mullah said, "Because in the house it is dark, out here it is so bright!"

We have looked for ourselves out here, but we will not be able to find ourselves until we look within, until we turn inside where it is dark.

Let us practise silence every day, preferably at the same time and at the same place — for this is our daily appointment with our own selves, our True Self, the Real Self, the Self Supreme that, for want of a better word, we call God. Begin with fifteen minutes, then gradually increase the period to at least one hour. At first, the practice may appear to be meaningless, a sheer waste of time. But if you persist in it, silence will become alive and the Word of God will speak to you. And you will realize that practising silence is, perhaps, the most worthwhile activity of the day.

In silence, let us pray, meditate, repeat the Name Divine, do our spiritual thinking, engage ourselves in a loving and intimate conversation with God.

Prayer is not a complicated affair. It is a very simple matter. It is as simple as talking to a friend. Suppose a friend visited you, it would be natural for you to discuss with him your ambitions and aspirations, your plans and programmes, your failures and frustrations, and to ask him to help you. Do likewise with God.

God is our one true, abiding Friend, the Friend of all friends. And God is available to us at all times. We do not have to go to a particular place to be able to contact God, for God is everywhere. All we have to do is to close our eyes, shut out the world, open our heart, call Him—and there He is in front of us! In the beginning, we will not be able to see Him. Let us be sure that He sees us. In the beginning, we will not be able to hear Him speak. Let us be sure that He hears us. A day will come when we, too, will see Him and hear Him speak.

A question is often asked, "If there is God and He is omnipresent, why can we not see Him?"

21

An amusing story is told to us in the *Talmud*, the Jewish scripture. It concerns the Emperor Hadrian who said to Rabbi Joshua, "You talk of God, but where is He? If He exists, can you show Him to me?"

"That is impossible," answered the Rabbi.

The Emperor insisted, "How can I believe in God when I cannot see Him?"

The Rabbi took the Emperor outside. It was a hot summer day. The Rabbi said, "Look at the sun."

"I cannot," answered the Emperor.

And the Rabbi said, "If you cannot even look at the sun, which is but a servant of God, how can you look at God Himself?"

Yes, God can be seen and heard. He is more real than all the things that we perceive with our outer senses.

To be able to see God, we have to put in effort. This effort is cultivating deep longing for the Lord, deep yearning for the First and only Fair. As Sri Ramakrishna said, "Long for the Lord even as a lover yearns for his beloved, as a miser yearns for gold, as a child yearns for his mother." Yearn for the Lord. Say to Him with tear-touched eyes, "I need You, Lord! I need nothing else – neither pleasures, nor possessions, nor power! I need You and You alone!" When God gets the assurance that you truly need Him and nothing besides, He will reveal Himself to you.

Think of God in any Form that draws you. He is the Formless One, but for the sake of His devotees, He has worn many Forms and visited the earth-plane again and again. Call Him by any Name that appeals to you. He is the Nameless One, though the sages have called Him by many Names. Do not quarrel over Forms or Names. You stick to the one that draws you: let others stick to the one that draws them. All Forms and Names ultimately lead to the One Who is beyond form and the formlessness. "On whatever path men approach Me," says the Lord in the Gita, "on that I go to meet them – for all the paths are Mine, verily Mine!"

We need to cultivate love – and longing – of the heart. And, therefore, we pray again and again to develop this love for God. Offer set prayers, if you will: but let your prayers emerge out of the very depths of a love-filled heart. "I love You, God! I want to love You, more and more! I want to love You more than anything in the world! I want to love You to distraction, to intoxication. Grant me pure love and devotion for Your Lotus Feet, and so bless me that this world-bewitching *maya* (the negative power; illusion) may not lead me astray. And so bless me, Blessed Master, that I may be an instrument of Thy help and healing in this world of suffering and pain."

When such a prayer emerges out of the very depths of a love-filled heart, the eyes are touched with tears and the mind does not wander. So many, alas, pray with their lips but their mind is distracted!

A holy man driving a car, met a beggar on the way. The beggar exclaimed, "If only I too, became a holy man, a man of prayer, I would have a car!"

"Prayer is not that easy," said the holy man. If you say, *toon thakur tum pai ardaas*, with a concentrated mind, the car will belong to you!"

"That is wonderful," said the astonished beggar. Joining his hands and closing his eyes, he said the prayer aloud:

Toon thakur tum pai ardaas
Jeea pinda sabh teri raas....

Suddenly his eyes opened and he asked, "Shall I have a garage along with the car? Else where would I keep it?"

It has been truly said that God does not consider the arithmetic of your prayers (how many they are); or the rhetoric of your prayers (how elegant they are); or the music of your prayers (how melodious they are); or the logic of your prayers (how methodical they are); but the sincerity of your prayers – how heartfelt they are.

The idea is to contact God who is the Source of health and happiness and success. Go to the Source if you wish to succeed in life. Make God real to yourself in daily life. Do not let Him be a far-off shadowy Being. Make Him a partner in your daily life. And be assured that there is no problem that God and you cannot solve together. There is no situation that God and you cannot handle together. There is no burden that God and you cannot lift together.

St. Teresa wanted to build an orphanage. She had only three shillings. She said to those who ridiculed her, "With three shillings Teresa can do nothing, but with God and three shillings, there is nothing that Teresa cannot do!"

The man whose hair stands on end at the mere mention of the Name of God, and from whose eyes flow tears of love – he has indeed reached his last birth.

Sri Ramakrishna Parmahansa

We must detoxicate ourselves from *maya* and enter into another kind of intoxication. We must lose ourselves — nay, drown ourselves — in the intoxication of God's love.

Such a one will find himself shedding unbidden tears of love and longing for the true and only Beloved.

J. P. V.

The Treasure Of Tears

Very many people who meet me tell me that they face one major problem when they start to meditate – the wandering mind.

"We close our eyes and sit in silence," they say, "but our mind wanders. And it's not just that the mind will not be still; we get such thoughts as would never disturb us otherwise, when we are at our routine work. However, when we try to enter into silence, they come to bother us. Why does this happen?"

Our minds are prone to distraction. Truly has it been said that the mind is a monkey; it wanders from one object to another, from one form to another. When we are at work we do not realize the restlessness, the fickleness of the mind. But when we sit in silence – the mind begins to play its tricks. It wanders, and we too, wander with it.

What can you do to stop the wandering mind in its tracks? What can you do to train the mind in *ekagrita* — one-pointed focus?

One of the best ways I know to control the wandering mind, is to develop love for God. As we all know, when we love something or someone deeply, our mind constantly gravitates towards that person. We have to apply the same principle to *abhyasa* — cultivate love for God in our hearts.

I truly believe that concentration is not possible until we awaken love in our hearts – the utmost love for God.

There are experts and practitioners who insist that *abhyasa* is based on emotionless detachment; and that God need not have anything to do with meditation. But I am firmly of the belief that for the beginner, love for God can be the greatest motivating, inspiring, uplifting factor.

Therefore, begin your *abhyasa* by developing love for God. And one mark of love is tears!

Have you ever shed tears for the love of the Lord? If you haven't, you cannot experience the bliss of loving Him.

What do tears have to do with love, you may ask. Have you seen how children cry when their mothers have to leave them for one reason or the other? It is not that they cry because they are unhappy — they cry because they love their mother so much that they cannot bear to be parted from her.

We must realize that we too, are children who have been parted from our Divine Mother. We have become separated from God, our true Beloved. Alas, this is a truth that very few of us are aware of—that we are in a state of separation from the Beloved. When this realization dawns on us, we begin to shed tears.

Most of us are so caught up in the entanglements of this world. We are so enslaved by what the world has given us — pleasure, possessions and power — that we do not even feel the need for God. How then can we shed tears for Him?

It is only after much wandering that this realization dawns on man — that he is living a life of separation from God. He may then begin to feel that his wandering has taken him so far away from God—and this will bring tears to His eyes.

It is then that he decides that he must begin his journey *back* to God, for this is the only journey that will make his life worthwhile. When he embarks on this journey, out of the depths of his heart will arise the cry: "Beloved, take the wanderer home!" and the tears begin to flow...

Rabia was once asked, "How do you worship God? Do you wait for God to enter your consciousness and then begin your prayer? Or is it the other way round—you begin your prayer and then God enters your heart?"

Rabia replied, "I do neither of these things. When my eyes are moist, when tears of love and longing flow from my eyes, I see God before me."

The way of *abhyasa* is not a mechanical sequence in which you "switch on" your worship and God appears on demand. Alas, our hearts and minds are not 'programmable'. It is likely that when you sit down to meditate, you will find your mind wrapped up in several layers. These layers need to be removed. It is therefore advisable to begin the meditation session with a *bhajan* or *kirtan* which will help to bring about the right mood and right feeling of devotion to take you further.

For some of us the right feeling, the right state of mind is more difficult to attain. If your hearts are so hardened that they cannot melt in love and devotion, then ask God, beg God to pour His grace on you so that you too, can cry out to Him, "Lord, take the wanderer Home!"

I said to you earlier that many of us remain trapped in the entanglements of the world. This is true of every *sansari jeev*—he is intoxicated with the pleasures, possessions and powers of this world. He is intoxicated with worldly love and longing—for *I, Me* and *Mine.*

He must detoxify himself of this *maya* and enter into another kind of intoxication—he must lose himself, nay, drown himself in the intoxication of God's love. Such a one will find himself shedding unbidden tears of love and longing for the true and only Beloved.

You can enter into this state of divine intoxication in the *satsang*, or at the feet of a holy one. Get detoxicated from *maya* – enter into the realm of the beloved in the company of the saints and sages!

Every saint wishes that his true disciples should develop two qualities – *viveka* and *vairagya*.

Viveka is the power of discrimination that helps us to distinguish between the real and the unreal, between *sat* and *asat*. When we attain *viveka* we will realize that what we have been chasing all our life are shadow-shapes, illusions that will not stay with us forever. *Viveka* will lead us on to *vairagya* – the spirit of dispassionate detachment. For if this earth is a shadow, how can we build upon it? What is there that we can be attached to in this world of transience?

Earlier, I spoke of tears — I meant tears that are born out of *viveka* and *vairagya*. Such tears are like the clean and pure Ganga that fell from Heaven, as a result of Bhagiratha's *tapasya;* this Ganga will purify you, cleanse you and set you in the right frame of mind, in the right attitude for *abhyasa*. Allow the tears to flow therefore; let them cleanse you, and then they will stop, when you are ready. And in this state you will feel that God is not from you afar. He is not locked up somewhere in a far-off temple; you do not have to go to a *tapovan* (forest of meditation) or a mountain-peak to find Him. He is *here*—He is *now*—He is in the heart within you. You can speak to Him, commune with Him as with a friend or with a member of your own family. Establish contact with Him in silence, and be prepared to LISTEN – for in the depths of silence will you hear His Divine Voice; not in the clamour and noise of this world.

A man who chooses the path of freedom from restraint, i.e. self-indulgence, will be a bond slave of passions, whilst the man who binds himself to rules and restraints releases himself.

Mahatma Gandhi

Freedom is not that you can do what you like. Freedom is to be able to do what you ought to do, what you should do.

J. P. V.

Self-Discipline Is The Key!

In the Hindu way of life, *yoga, dhyana* and *abhyasa* are almost used as synonyms of *sadhana* or spiritual practice. *Sadhana* is nothing but the spiritual discipline that is achieved by repeating the same activity (*kriya*) systematically.

I spoke earlier of the need to be in the right frame of mind, to cleanse the heart of the impurities that clog our beings. The Hindu way of life recommends certain *yamas* and *niyamas* – restraints and observances – to help us attain a state of inner purification.

I would describe *yamas* and *niyamas* as an impregnable armour that protects the aspirants as he sets out on the path of *abhyasa*.

What are *yamas* and *niyamas*? In simple terms, they constitute a code of conduct which enables us to live a successful life in moral and spiritual terms. We are indeed fortunate that the Hindu scriptures give us such an ethical guideline to right thinking and right living. These restrictions and observances – moral and ethical Do's and Don'ts – give us the essence of our duties to ourselves and others, which are fundamental to a life of *dharma*. Maharishi Patanjali refers to them in two of his texts - *Yoga Darsana* and *Hatha Yoga Pradipika*.

In the context of *abhyasa, yamas* and *niyamas* have an added significance. In the common man's life, they help him lead a life of righteousness. In the life of an aspirant, they serve as aids to purification of the *antahkarna*, making *sadhana* easy and simple. Several of the obstacles on the path of *abhyasa* can be easily surmounted by adopting these.

The *yamas* or restraints are perhaps more difficult, for they require us to give up bad habits and negative traits that have become ingrained in us:

1. *Ahimsa* – Non-violence:

This involves non-violence in thought, word and deed. No living being must be harmed by our speech, thinking or action. An aspirant may not be able to live in solitude to achieve these ideals; but he must try to create an environment in which violence cannot be generated.

Violence is hatred and cruelty. Its antidote is love, which has the power to conquer the Universe!

Nagmahasaya is still remembered as the very personification of the principle of *ahimsa*. In his life, thoughts and words he held up the ideal: *Ahimsa Paro Dharma* — non-violence is the greatest virtue. His compassion extended to all creation. There was a pond next to his house, and during the rains, the overflow from the river brought hundreds of fishes to the pond. When fishermen came to net the fish, Nagmahasaya would pay them money to buy the fish back from them and put the struggling creatures back in the water where they could live.

So vigilant was he about the ideal of non-violence that he would not even allow poisonous snakes to be killed. One day, a venomous cobra entered the courtyard of his house. All the family members were

33

alarmed, and his wife called out, "Kill that creature at once!"

Nagmahasaya would not hear of it. "The snake of the forest can do us no harm; let us beware of the snake in the mind, which can really destroy our lives!" he said to his people. Then, approaching the deadly cobra with folded hands, he said: "Thou art the creature of the *vana devata*, the mistress of the Forest. May it please Thee to leave my humble cottage and return to Thy abode."

As people watched in amazement, he led the way out of his house and the snake followed him with his head bent, all the way to the jungle!

Nagmahasaya often said: "The outer world is nothing but a projection of the mind within. What you give out to the world, you will receive back from it."

My Beloved Master, Sadhu Vaswani, often said to us, "For me, not to love bird and beast would be not to love the Lord!" For he saw God's loving image reflected in every creature, every insect, every fish. Once, a swarm of bees had built their hive near his house. Afraid of their sting, some one suggested that the hive should be removed. "How can men and bees live together?" they demanded to know.

"Then let the men go!" was Sadhu Vaswani's quiet reply.

Sadhu Vaswani was also opposed to all forms of animal sacrifice. He taught us that the 'sacrifices' enjoined in the ancient scriptures were really symbolic and that the *real* sacrifice we have to offer, was to kill the animal *inside* us – animals like anger, jealousy, hatred and envy.

2. *Satya* – Truth:

Falsehood and lies corrupt life, although people constantly resort to "white lies" and flattery. It may be asked whether anyone can ever put into practice the ideal of speaking truth in its entirety at all times, in all places – truth, the whole truth and nothing but the truth. But the aspirant must practise truth to the extent of his capacity.

The observance of silence and the occasional choice of solitude can be beneficial to the practice of *satya*.

Socrates was one of the wisest men of the ancient world. Many were the youths whose lives he influenced for the better.

Socrates counselled his disciples to keep their mouths shut – and speak only when absolutely necessary.

"O wise one, how may we know when it is right to speak?" they asked him.

"Open your mouths to speak only after you have asked yourself three questions and received an affirmative answer to each of the three, replied Socrates.

What were the three questions?

The first question we must ask ourselves before we speak is – is it true? If we are not sure about the veracity of what we are saying, it is better that we do not utter a word. When we utter words carelessly, we ourselves become transmitters of untruth.

The second question to ask is – is it pleasant? Many are the empty remarks and vain statements that people make in idleness to hurt others. It is better that these unpleasant words remain unspoken.

The third question according to Socrates is – is it useful? Is our statement going to benefit the listener? Will our words bring comfort to someone? Are we likely to help someone with what we say? Only in that case should we go ahead and speak.

An Eastern account of Jesus attributes the following statement to him, "A day will come when you will have to render account for every idle word you have spoken."

We will all do well to remember this; we must pay – not merely for an untrue word, not merely for a bitter word, but for every *idle* word we have uttered!

Is it true? Is it pleasant? Is it useful? These are the three questions we must ask ourselves before we speak.

3. *Asteya* – Non-stealing:

At its best this is non-covetousness, that is, not coveting, seeking or even *wishing* to possess what belongs to another.

You have doubtless heard the story of the poor woodcutter who lost his axe, haven't you? You know how the fairy offered him a golden axe and a silver axe, which he refused because they were not his. When his old iron axe was given to him, he took it with gratitude: "Yes! This is my axe! Thank you for restoring it to me."

You know, too, the happy ending of the story: the fairy was so pleased with his honesty that she gave him the gold and silver axes, as her personal gifts!

Let me give you a modern, high-tech version of the story. This time, it is an intelligent, but simple, hardworking engineer, who is the hero of our story. He had been posted at the construction site of a huge dam. He was working on his own PC in his office by the river, when flash floods washed his office away, along with the computer.

Now the PC was an old, secondhand one which he had acquired with a whole month's salary, and he was naturally grieved over its loss. How would he ever get another PC at such a low price?

The *devta* of the river was moved by his grief and appeared before him with a brand new laptop. "Here is your computer," she said to him kindly. "Keep it!"

The poor engineer stared at the laptop in stupefaction. "But ..." he stammered. "Ma'am, you're making a mistake! This is a Sony VAIO – and mine was not a laptop...."

"Alright," said the *devta*, smiling to herself. She reappeared with a brand new Intel P-IV PC and said, "Here's your computer – it is a PC, as you can see."

"No Ma'am, no," protested our hero. "Why, this is a brand new, costly P-IV Computer! Mine was just an old, secondhand machine..."

"Alright, alright," sighed the *devta*, exasperated because she really wanted to be nice to the poor man – if only he would let her! "Don't fret," she added, seeing that he continued to be distressed. "Here you are – is this yours?"

The old, shabby PC with its worn out keyboard and shabby monitor appeared before our hero – and he was delighted. "Thank you, O, thank you, dear lady!" he gushed. "I really don't know how I would have managed without my PC. They don't give us one at work, you know," he added. "I bought this with my own money."

"Yes I *know*," snapped the *devta*, unable to hide her annoyance. "I wanted to give you a brand new computer, but you would not take it from me!"

"Oh Ma'am," said the engineer, appalled at the suggestion, "how could I possibly take something that was not mine?"

"Alright, alright," said the *devta*. "You've proved your point. Now take the other two anyway—I'm giving

37

them to you with my love and blessings. They are yours to keep!"

The engineer was overjoyed. With *three* computers now at his disposal, he quit his poorly paid job at the construction site and set up his own business as a consultant civil engineer.

A greedy friend, also an engineer, heard about the miraculous gift and decided to seek his fortune the same way. He got a job at the same site, set himself up at the same office, and bought an old, useless, non-functional PC for a few hundred rupees. When no one was looking, he threw the computer into the river one evening, and began to wail loudly.

"Alright, alright," said the *devta*, appearing before him. "What's wrong?" (She did not know what was up, you see, because she was not responsible for the loss of the PC.)

"My PC! My PC!" sobbed the crafty engineer. "Oh what will I do without it? It fell into the river and was washed away. Oh Ma'am, you appear to be so kind and generous. Won't you make good my loss?"

"Fell into the river?" said the *devta* suspiciously. "Are you sure?"

"Sure, I am sure," swore the dishonest young man. "I am equally sure you are not going to leave me to face such a loss. So, can I have my PC back?"

In an instant, the wise *devta* understood the game the man was playing. "Sure, sure," she said, thinking furiously. In a moment, she produced an object which looked like a matchbox. "Is this it?" she asked him solicitously.

The engineer was disgusted. "No, of course not," he said rudely. "This is some tinderbox and not a PC at all!"

The 'matchbox' vanished and a little pocket book now appeared in the hands of the *devta*. "Is this what you lost?"

Now the engineer decided to make his move. "See Ma'am," he said, "You are obviously not able to find my PC. So, why don't you give me a new laptop or something instead? I don't mind accepting a different computer from you!"

"You thief, you dishonest rogue," said the *devta*, gnashing her teeth. "Not only did you covet another new PC, but you were also too stupid to realise that what I showed you were the latest palm-top versions. Now here is your old, useless PC, which you dumped into the river. You can keep it with my compliments."

This story may make you smile. But it should also make you realise that covetousness is now taking newer forms; when we crave for other's possessions, or indeed, we want to *make* quick money without earning it, working for it, we taint ourselves with the sin of 'stealing' as much as any thief.

4.   *Brahmacharya* – Celibacy:

Literally translated, *brahmacharya* means walking with God. In practical terms we associate this with celibacy, continence in thought, word and deed.

To my young readers, male and female, this might be an ideal that is impossible to achieve. But let me assure them, that it is both possible and attainable.

Sexual energy and vigour continue to accumulate in the male and female body from childhood. Yet in childhood, this energy is preserved and not squandered away. The ideal therefore, is to attain such a state of childlike innocence and simplicity which will enable us to uphold this difficult, but not impossible ideal.

Physics and aeronautics have made it possible for a jumbo jet, weighing thousands of tons, to take off and fly in the sky, with hundreds of passengers. Space research has enabled us to send up 'shuttle' flights that cross and re-cross the gravitational barriers and operate space-labs in the realm of weightlessness. So too, it is possible to attain to complete celibacy with the help of the science of *yoga*. Our great Maharishis like Narada, Suka and Sanaka have set wonderful examples for us in this regard. Conserving sexual energy and sublimating sexual desire, one can really elevate one's consciousness.

Literally and metaphorically, the story of sage Vishwamitra illustrates the necessity for *brahmacharya*, especially in serious aspirants.

Sage Vishwamitra was engaged in the most austere *tapasya* that would make him a *brahma rishi*. Determined to succeed in his endeavour, he withstood hunger, thirst and all bodily needs, focusing his heart, mind and soul on the Almighty.

Fearful of his power, the *devas* sent the beautiful danseuse from *Indraloka*, called Menaka, to distract him from his penance.

Alas, the sage who had risen above all physical needs, succumbed to the desire of the flesh, *kama*. He lost his power of self-control when he beheld the beautiful danseuse. He gave up his *tapasya* to be with her – and out of this union was born the ill-fated Shakuntala, who had to suffer rejection and humility, before she could attain her rightful place by the side of her husband, Dushyanta.

These stories from our *Puranas* are meant to teach us truths which we should imbibe and adopt in our own lives. You know too, the story of Bhishma from the *Mahabharata* – his father's *kama*, passion for the fisherwoman Satyavati, was responsible for denying Bhishma his birthright to succeed his father, denying the *Kuru* dynasty of someone who would have been a wonderful ruler! It is another matter, that Bhishma became the ideal exponent of *brahmacharya*, a *yogi* who worked out his *karmic* destiny and attained *mukti*.

5. *Aparigraha* – Non-possession:

The natural human tendency is to accumulate possessions. Greater and smaller needs, perceived needs and felt needs prompt us to acquire more and more things. Possessions take us far, far away from the ideals of simplicity and non-covetousness.

Airlines are quite strict in restricting passengers to carry only a specific quantity of baggage, subject to strict checks. "Excess baggage" is charged heavily. Too many possessions in life are also excess baggage on the seeker's path. *Aparigraha* is one restraint that prevents the mind from focus and concentration, and allows it to wander at will.

Sadhu Vaswani was the very embodiment of *aparigraha*. At one time, while he was in Hyderabad—Sind, he lived in the 'Hari Mandir', a big hall in which a mattress was spread on one side. He slept on the mattress at night, and, during the day, he sat on it to do his work. There was a small desk on which he did his writing. The many books he loved to read were spread all around.

One day, a Frenchman came to visit him. He had learnt of Sadhu Vaswani through the writings of Mon. Paul Richard, who had met him earlier, and had carried away an unforgettable impression. Mon. Paul Richard had written, "I have been blessed, for amidst the deserts of Sind, I have found a true Prophet, a Messenger of the new Spirit – a saint, a sage and a seer, a *rishi* of new India, a leader of the great future – Sadhu Vaswani."

The Frenchman, used to the ways of the world, expected to see Sadhu Vaswani living in an impressive residence, with a well-furnished office of his own. He was astonished to see the saint dwelling in a corner of a simple hall, with a mattress, a low desk and some books.

Unable to overcome his surprise, he asked Sadhu Vaswani, "Where is your furniture?"

"Where is yours?" smiled the sage.

"My furniture is in my home in France," said the visitor. "I am only a traveler here!"

Softly, Sadhu Vaswani answered, "So am I!"

How true are his words! "Take no luggage with thee, O, traveler to the Temple of the Beloved! Tread thou the Path, empty-handed! And when thou wilt reach the Temple, thou wilt know that the empty alone are filled."

6.   *Kshama* – Forgiveness and Forbearance:

We tend to love and praise those who do good to us, while we hate and revile those who harm us. It is important to avoid both extremes of attraction and aversion if we wish the mind to attend serenity and tranquillity.

Mahatma Gandhi was nearly slain by a fanatic in 1908. Gandhiji refused to testify against him. "He is not aware of what he has done," the Mahatma pointed out to those who wished to prosecute him. "He must be won over by love and compassion."

Sure enough, the man was acquitted, as Gandhiji refused to give evidence against him. After a year, he wrote to Gandhiji, apologising profoundly for his deed, and expressing his admiration for the Mahatma.

"An eye for an eye would only leave all the world half-blind," Mahatma Gandhi once remarked. It was the quality of *kshama* – forgiveness and forbearance, which helped him perfect the indomitable, unconquerable weapon of *satyagraha*. He did not hate the British or blame them personally, his objection was to their policies and principles.

7. *Dhriti* – Steadfastness:

What may I tell you about the great ideal which enjoins us to rise above inertia, indecision and changeability? Truly, he who practises *dhriti* is the dearest devotee of the Lord, and his qualities are outlined by Sri Krishna in the *Bhagavad Gita*:

- He is free from ill-will and egoism; he is poised in pain and pleasure.
- He is content and balanced in harmony, his mind and understanding dedicated to the Lord.
- He does not disturb the world, nor is he disturbed by the world.
- He is without ambition; he is free from passion and fear.
- He does not rejoice, grieve or crave for anything.
- He is the same to foe and friend. He is the same in honour and dishonour. He is free from attachment.
- He takes praise and blame alike. He is satisfied with whatever the Lord is pleased to grant him.

The Bhagavad Gita cites King Janaka as the perfect example of *dhriti* or steadfastness. There is a beautiful story told to us of Janaka, who once went to the *ashrama* of Rishi Sukha, and asked to be accepted as a disciple along with the other students already there – for great was his aspiration to learn spiritual truths.

Janaka's presence in the *ashram* made the other disciples envious. They felt that their *guru* was showing him special favours. They went so far as to accuse their *guru* of favouritism – all because Janaka was a King, while they were ordinary folk.

The Rishi tried to explain to them that it was Janaka's devotion and piety that he valued, but they were not convinced.

One day, in the midst of an important lesson, panic broke out in the *ashrama* as people began to shout that the city of Mithila was on fire. The concentration of the class was shattered, and the Rishi had to break off his lesson, midway.

"Would you like to go into the city and see to your families?" he asked the disciples. "Janaka, would you like to go and make sure all is well with the palace?"

"All will happen as God wills," replied Janaka. "Pray, let me continue to hear your *upadesh*." He refused to move from his seat at the feet of the *guru*.

As for the others, they fled helter-skelter, worried about their homes and possessions. When they reached Mithila, they found that there was no fire – the entire 'event' had been created by the *guru* to put his pupils to the test. When they returned to the *ashram* they found Janaka, focused as always, carefully listening to the *guru's* teachings, unperturbed, unmoved, calm as calm could be.

"One disciplined student is worth a hundred unstable minds," the *guru* said to them. "I value Janaka for his equanimity, not for his royal birth!"

8. *Daya* – Compassion:

This is the quality that makes a human being assert his 'superiority' over the rest of creation – not his power, his strength or his intelligence – but his capacity for compassion. Not only does he practise non-violence, but goes out of his way to alleviate the pain and misery of other creatures – human and non-human. Compassion arises out of *sattvic* qualities, and makes us beautiful *within*.

When we grow in the awareness that we are members of the larger family of creation, we learn to live up to the ancient Indian ideal, *Vasudaiva Kutumbakam*—this whole world, this vast universe, this unexplored cosmos with its magnificent creation is ONE family. And we realise that these hands are given us to bless, not to butcher! These hands are given to us to save, not to slaughter!

Shibi was a great King of ancient India. He was known as a kind and charitable ruler, who was the very soul of compassion. Wishing to put Shibi to the test, Indra and Agni formulated a plan. Agni took on the form of a dove and Indra took on the form of a fierce hawk. They flew into the palace of the King.

Shibi was busy distributing alms to the poor, as was his daily wont. Suddenly a terrified dove plunged down on to his wrist and looked at him appealingly. Overhead, the cruel hawk circled, waiting to get at its prey.

Shibi stroked the dove lovingly. "Rest, gentle bird," he said. "You will not come to harm while you are with me."

The hawk flew down as if to attack the King and snatch the dove away. But the King raised his hand and obstructed the hawk.

45

"This dove is my prey, O, King," the hawk said. "I have been pursuing this dove since morning. Why do you try to rob me of my food?"

The King was taken aback to hear the hawk speak thus. However, he replied, "This poor dove has taken refuge at my hands. It is my duty to protect her from all harm. Under no circumstance will I allow you to harm her or make her your prey."

"You are indeed the soul of kindness, O, King," the hawk said to him haughtily. "But is your kindness limited to protecting the dove? Am I not entitled to a share of your compassion? By depriving me of food, aren't you being cruel to me? What kind of *dharma* is this that you practise?"

King Shibi was shocked. Not only could the hawk speak like a human being—but he could also argue like a sophist!

"Let me assure you, hawk," he said, "I will provide for your hunger. But you must let the poor dove go."

"So what will you give me instead? I can only consume flesh, and you know it. Will you kill another bird to provide for me?"

"Certainly not," said the King. "I shall offer you my own flesh instead."

"I will accept it provided you give me flesh exactly equal to the weight of the dove," the hawk replied.

"So it shall be," the King assured him. And so, he ordered his servants to bring a balance. The dove was placed on one side; with his own sword, the King cut off a piece of flesh from his arm and placed it on the other side.

The dove had looked frail. But the flesh cut off from the King could not equal its weight. So, Shibi went on cutting more and more flesh from his body and placing it on the balance.

It was of no avail. Giving up the attempt, a tired and bleeding Shibi threw away the sword and himself sat on the balance. As if by magic, the balance stood still.

"Behold, O hawk, I offer you my flesh, exactly equal to the dove. Please eat me — but spare the life of the dove."

As he said these words, the gods showered flowers from the heavens. In an instant, Indra and Agni assumed their original forms and stood before Shibi in all their celestial splendour.

"God save you, King!" they exclaimed. "You have indeed proved yourself to be great. We offer you our apologies for putting you to such a test. May you be richly blessed!"

They touched Shibi, and in an instant, his wounds were healed, and he became strong and whole again. The Gods blessed him and returned to their abode.

To this day, Shibi is regarded as the supreme example of compassion. We may not equal him in courage and spirit, but surely we can draw inspiration from his example!

9. *Arjava* – Simplicity:

Nowadays, everyone is talking about raising their standard of living. When one has got a car and an apartment, one looks for a weekend cottage or a farmhouse; when one grows bored with vacations in India, one hopes to take vacations in Europe and America. More, More, More – is the *mantra* for many. How could they then understand Thoreau's clarion call: Simplify! Simplify! Simplify!

47

The trouble with modern life is that it has become too complex, too difficult, too overcrowded. People rush through packed days attending committee meetings, keeping appointments, meeting deadlines and chalking out more programmes. Social obligations, children's activities, professional concerns and personal finances make their own demands. At the end of the day men and women complain, "I'm exhausted! I've been rushed off my feet!"

The tendency is to blame it all on *life*, on the *world*, on our *working environment*. But the problem of complexity is not external or environmental. When there is integrity of the Self within, external complications will not affect us.

Did you hear the story of the American millionaire who wanted to "get away from it all" and travelled to the South Sea Islands for a quiet and relaxing holiday? Once he got to his Island paradise, he spent the first three days giving instructions to his business manager, his stock broker, his accountant and his lawyer – and left the following day because he could not find the peace and relaxation that he was looking for! He was carrying his own complications with him. How could he hope to get rid of them in Hawaii or Bali?

When Mahatma Gandhi was to go to Bengal to serve the famine-stricken people, his assistants reserved two Third-Class compartments for the exclusive use of his party of volunteers.

On arriving at the station, Gandhi found that two compartments were not needed; with a little adjustment, everyone could be fitted into one of them.

He called his son, and asked him to vacate the second compartment and inform the railway authorities accordingly.

"But *Bapuji*," the son protested. "Both compartments have been reserved for us! And we have already paid the railway authorities for both."

"That does not matter at all," Gandhiji replied. "Do remember we are going to Bengal for the service of the poor and starving millions. How can we enjoy the luxury and comfort of so much space while we are on such a mission? And besides, see for yourself, the suffocating rush and overcrowding in the other Third-Class compartments. Why should we occupy more space than we need? It is a crime to waste seats just because we have 'reserved' them!"

No further arguments were heard. The volunteers vacated their seats in the second compartment and crowded into one compartment. Only then was Gandhiji able to relax.

It was this utter simplicity of Gandhiji that stole the hearts of thousands of British workers when he went to England for a crucial Round Table Conference. An arrogant Churchill may have described him as a "half naked *fakir*", but the common British people took him to their hearts, for in his simplicity and utterly unpretentious attitude, he was one of them, their admired friend and role model!

10. *Mitahara* – Moderation in appetite:

We eat to live – but many of us make *eating* the primary object of life. Some people demand specific foods, delicacies and endless variety. Yet others gorge on junk foods that only add toxicity to their system. Food has become an unhealthy obsession for some.

Ideally, food should be consumed as *Prasad* coming to us out of God's kindness. We should eat a digestible, *sattvic* meal with gratitude to God, leaving the stomach one-fourth empty – this is indeed *Mitahara*.

Overeating is one of the surest deterrents to *sadhana*.

11. *Saucha* – Purity:

Remember, purity is both external and internal. Bathing with expensive soap, with water to which antiseptics are added, and using clean, new clothes is not what purity is all about. Yes, the body is the temple of the indwelling *atman*, and it must be maintained well. But the purity of the *antahkarna* is far more important.

Our ancient scriptures identify four aspects of the *antahkarna* or inner instrument: *chitta* (mind stuff), *manas* (mind), *buddhi* (intellect) and *ahankara* (egoism). How can this complex entity be kept pure?

The answer is simple: through penance, reading of the scriptures and association with the wise and holy ones. When the inner instrument is purified, our words and actions too, are purified. Evil thoughts are eradicated by the presence of wise and holy ones, and we emerge as cleaner, purer beings ready to undertake the spiritual pilgrimage of *abhyasa*.

Have you heard the story of the monk and the courtesan? An ascetic lived on a street near the temple, to which hundreds of devotees went everyday. They passed before the ascetic who sat outside his home, ostensibly meditating. But he hardly saw these pious souls. His eyes were constantly fixed on the house opposite, where a courtesan lived. He gnashed his teeth in rage and fury, as he saw her 'customers' come and go. Every morning, without fail, the courtesan would go to the temple: every time she returned, the monk would get up from his special seat and thunder at her,

"Repent, repent, you wretched woman! Mend your ways before it is too late – for the fires of hell await you!"

Years later, the monk and the courtesan died on the same day, at the same time. As their souls mounted to heaven, the angels came to receive the courtesan and take her to *swargaloka*—heaven. As for the monk, he was shown the way to *naraka*, hell.

"This is preposterous," he protested. "You take this filthy, immoral sinner to heaven, while I, a pure, evolved soul am condemned to enter hell? How is this to be tolerated?"

"Here in heaven, we judge souls by the purity within, not outer purity," the angels replied. "This woman lived a life of immorality, but her heart and mind were ever pure, ever focussed on the Lord. As for you, you practised austerity and penance, but your mind and heart were filled with impure thoughts. While she thought of the Lord and of Him alone, you thought of *her* and the men who came to her. How could you describe yourself as pure?"

The man was abashed. He realised his mistake, and resolved to think and act for better *karma* in his next birth.

The flowering of love is meditation.

Jiddu Krishnamurti

Meditation is directing our attention
to the Eternal and keeping it there
for a while.

J. P. V.

What Is Meditation?

The word "meditation" is derived from the Latin root which means "to heal".

Some scholars say that the root of the word 'meditation' is similar to the root of medicine and medicate – which means 'paying attention to' something. When we meditate, we pay attention to those depths in our being which are not known to the people outside – which are, perhaps not familiar even to ourselves! Thus meditation has been described as a process of inner attention.

Psychiatrists as well as spiritual teachers now agree that there are three states of consciousness in all of us: the conscious mind with which all of us are familiar; the subconscious, which is the hidden but powerful part of our psyche, with which we connect only during sleep; the superconscious which represents the highest degree of awareness that we are capable of. It is the source of the brightest light, the highest power of which we are capable. Meditation is the process in which we establish contact with our superconsciousness.

We live in a world of allurements and entanglements. The sharp arrows of desire, craving, animal appetite, of passion and pride, of ignorance and anger, of hatred and greed, wound our souls, again and again. Our souls bear the scars of many wounds: they need to be healed. Silence is the great healer. We must take a dip every day in the waters of silence if we wish to be healed, cleansed, ennobled and strengthened for the daily tasks of life.

While many regard meditation as a difficult art, in itself it is so simple. Meditation is directing our attention to the Eternal and keeping it there for a while. Within every one of us is a realm of peace, power, perfection. Through practice, we can, at will, enter this realm and contact God. When we do so, we become conscious of infinite power, a wondrous peace, and realise that everything is perfect and in its own place.

To know what meditation is, we need to go within ourselves and, in the words of Sadhu Vaswani, "sink deeper and deeper". No one else can do that for us; we need to do it ourselves. We need to strip ourselves of all pride and passion, selfishness, sensuality and sluggishness of soul. We need to remove veil after veil until we reach the inmost depths and touch the Pure White Flame.

This demands that we throw the dirt out of our mind. One is as one thinks, taught the great *Rishis* of ancient India. Therefore, let us take care of our thoughts.

"The mind," Bishop Fulton J. Sheen once said, "is like a clock that is constantly running down and must be wound up daily with good thoughts." Fill the mind with noble thoughts. The minds of many, I am afraid, are full of unwholesome thoughts and wrong ideas. It is such thoughts that do not let us live a healthy, happy and successful life.

Often, we pay scant attention to our thoughts. We say, "After all, it was but a thought." But we must never forget that thoughts are things, thoughts are forces, thoughts are the building blocks of life. With thoughts we are building the edifice of our own life, building our own future. People blame their stars, their destiny. "Men heap together the mistakes of their lives," said John Oliver Hobbes, "and create a monster they call destiny." Destiny is not a matter of chance: it is a matter of choice.

We are building our own destiny, everyday, with the thoughts that we think. A thought, if it is constantly held in the mind, will drive us to action. An action that is repeated creates a habit. It is our habits that form our character. And it is character that determines our destiny.

So if we wish to change our destiny, we must begin by changing our pattern of thinking. We must cleanse the mind of all the dirt that we have accumulated through the years. Our minds need to be cleansed of thoughts of lust, hatred, greed, passion and pride, selfishness and miserliness, avarice and arrogance, envy and jealousy, resentment and ill-will.

Like all spiritual experiences, meditation is something that cannot come to us from without. It is true, that in the early stages of our spiritual unfolding, the *exterior* life, in a large measure, does shape the interior life. What we think and feel, what we read and hear, what we do and speak during the day, is echoed within us in the hours of silence. So it is that we must take the greatest care of our *outer* life. We must keep a watch over our thoughts and feelings, our aspirations and desires, our words and deeds.

Meditation is gazing inward by opening another aperture of the mind. It is turning away from all outer objects to seek Him whom the Rishis call *Ekamevadvityam* — the One without a second, the One and only Reality. Meditation is entering upon the interior pilgrimage in which layer after layer of unreality is to be torn. The pilgrim, therefore, proceeds by negation: *neti, neti,* not this, not this! These are not God: I seek Him alone!

The pilgrim enters, more and more, into silence. In silence, he understands the secrets of true freedom. In silence, he makes the discovery that he is not a creature bounded by space and time. He is a child of Eternity: and Eternity is here and now. He is not the isolated creature he thought himself to be. He is a "wave of the unbounded deep". He is one with all life, all creation. He is in all: all are in Him!

As we sit in silence, let us think of a world that is very much like this world but that is free of all disorder and chaos – a world in which everything is done for love's sake, where everyone else, where everything comes to pass in the right way, at the right time, in a perfectly harmonious manner. As we do this, we will find the perfection and peace of God flowing into our lives like a perennial river.

Meditation is not an achievement or distinction that we seek to add to our credit rating. The only reason we choose to meditate is to fulfill a deep thirst, a powerful aspiration in us. The wealth and values of this world do not give us the peace we crave. Worldly achievements and success do not give us a true sense of fulfillment. Like Goethe, we call out, "Light! More Light!" Meditation leads us to the Light of all lights.

Let me also warn you, meditation is not mere escapism. If we wish to run away from our responsibilities, duties, commitments and obligations, as well as our problems and sufferings, meditation is not the answer. Our frustrations and failures and disappointments will not equip us to take on the spiritual discipline that meditation requires.

Meditation is a process of self-awakening through which we connect ourselves to God. *Dhyana Yoga*, as it is called is nothing but establishing our rightful union with God, as God's children. It enables us to be receptive to God's voice, which can only be heard in inner stillness. In His voice is true Wisdom; in His message to us is true Peace. Meditation leads us on to this Divine Peace.

Meditation is not the same as reflection, contemplation or introspection – though all of these may be useful aids in preparing for meditation. Some people even spend hours with closed eyes, fantasizing; or stare vacantly with open eyes, daydreaming. These are certainly not to be confused with meditation.

Some people describe meditation as an art; others call it a science. It would be truer to say that it is a process or technique by which we link ourselves with the highest state of "awareness" or "consciousness" that we can reach.

Meditation is the best way to attain self-knowledge which is perhaps the highest 'knowledge' that man can aspire to. By self-knowledge I do not mean a SWOT analysis of your personality – but an introduction to your true self. When you know yourself, you realise your potential and widen your possibilities. Therefore, meditation can also be an effective instrument to help you transform your life by enriching your creativity, and adding to your sense of harmony and power of happiness.

Meditation is not strenuous or difficult or complicated; when it is practised under proper guidance, it is a peaceful, relaxing process which helps ease stress of body and mind. Therefore, meditation is therapeutic even during its earliest stages. It is the best antidote to stress and tension.

Meditation is not an 'interior monologue' or an inner conversation with yourself. It is not even a system of thought-clarification or seeking solution to a problem. Rather, it is an effort to achieve single-minded, one-pointed focus of awareness – what the Gita describes as *ekagrita*.

Meditation is not emptying the mind of all thoughts—for that is impossible for us to achieve. Rather, through meditation, we try to focus our mind on a single point or object which will enable us to reach deeper into our superconsciousness. In this process of unitary focus, relief is automatically brought to the mind from its habitual stresses, strains and tensions.

Meditation disciplines the mind, sharpens concentration and improves memory. It also energises body and mind. Thus modern medical practioners have begun to use it as an effective aid in healing and therapy.

Meditation also helps the mind to relate to our inner instinct – intuition, as it is called. This connection aids our creativity and innovative thinking. Thus meditation is a systematic method of tapping human brilliance.

In this journey to the Uttermost, it is helpful to have the grace and guidance of a Godman or a friend of God – someone who lives and moves and has his being in God. Him we call a Teacher, a Guru. An Enlightened One, a Man of Light Sadhu Vaswani often said to us, is better than a thousand men who may have read thousands of books. If we would enter into the Secret of Life — the Secret that is God — we must go and seek someone who is pure and holy and free. Through his grace, we will find it easy to tread the Path which the *Upanishads* have called the "razor's edge".

To grow in the inner life, the life of the Spirit, we need to withdraw from the outer world of noise and excitement. Each day, we must spend some time – at least an hour – in silence. At the very start, perhaps, it will be difficult to sit in silence for an hour at a stretch. Then it would be well if we practise silence for about a quarter of an hour, four times a day.

Sitting in silence, what do we find? We may have selected a silence corner in a garden or on a riverbank, far from the madding crowds of men and motorcars. But, as we go and sit there, we find that we are overwhelmed by a new type of noise. For noise is of two types: (1) exterior; and (2) interior. It is easy to keep away from outer noise. There are silence spots in every place, where the din and roar of cities do not reach. But it is a difficult task to still the noise that is within – the clamour of conflicting thoughts.

A beautiful story is told us of Guru Nanak – a Great Master of the Silent Way. A *mullah* (Muslim priest) meets him and says to him, "You speak of the oneness of all faiths. You urge that the Hindu and the Muslim are both dear to God, whose children are we all. Then come with me and offer worship to Allah in the orthodox Muslim way: come and do *namaz* with me!"

The Guru readily consents: And the two go to a mosque: and the priest (the *mullah*) shows to the prophet (the Guru) the way to pray! The *mullah* inserts his fingers into his ears and kneels down to pray: the *mullah* goes through the ritual. The Guru keeps standing.

Then says the *mullah*, "Why are you standing there like a log of wood? Why don't you pray with me?"

59

Then the Guru smiles, and gently says, "My brother, if only you prayed, I, too, would pray with you! But, as your lips uttered the sacred words, your mind, alas, wandered to the stable where your mare is about to give birth to a foal. And you wondered about the colour of its skin! How you wished it were white as wool!"

So, it is with many of us. We sit in silence: with our lips we pray to God, but our minds, alas, stray to the stables of the world. Things and thoughts, to which we pay the least attention during waking hours, rise out of nowhere, and, like swarms of mosquitoes, disturb our peace. The more we try to brush them aside, the more formidable they become.

What shall I do? Do nothing. Let me but sit still, as a silent spectator viewing the shifting scenes of a fickle mind. Let me but sit as, years ago, I sat in a theatre watching a play. The actors appeared on the stage, played their respective roles, then disappeared: I kept looking on! So, too, let me keep looking on at the thoughts that rush out of the unknown deep in a seemingly endless procession. They are not my thoughts. I have nought to do with them. They come: let them come. They will soon pass out, leaving the chamber of my mind cleaner and brighter than before. They are the dirt and filth that have accumulated within the cells of my mind during a lifetime, or, maybe, during many long ages. If the dirt and filth are washed off, I have every reason to rejoice. The bad odour that is let out in the process should neither frighten me nor disquiet my mind.

In due course, the mind will become calm and clear as the surface of a lake on a windless day. Such a mind will become a source of indescribable joy and peace.

Significant are the words of the *Upanishad*: "The mind alone is the cause of man's bondage: the mind is also an instrument of man's liberation."

To sit in silence, I must learn to be still — to do nothing. "The more a man does," says an English mystic, "the more he is and exists. And the more he is and exists, the less of God is and exists within him." To be still, I must learn the art of separating myself from the changing moods of the mind, from its flights, which are faster by far than the fastest supersonic jets.

One simple exercise will be very helpful. Let me imagine the mind in the form of a room. In this room let me select a corner and sweep it clean. Then let me sit in the corner and quietly watch the antics and acrobatics of the mind. If only I can dissociate myself from them, I shall have thrown off the yoke of the mind. I shall have broken the tyranny of the "ego", which is the only hurdle between me and my God: I shall have grown into that true awareness that, in the midst of my daily duties, I have kept my heart fixed on the One Divine Reality.

Yet another exercise can be found very helpful. As I sit in silence, let me offer my mind at the Lotus Feet of the Lord. Everytime I find the mind flying off on a tangent, let me quickly and gently bring it back to the Lotus Feet of the Lord. If, for a whole hour, I have done no more than bring the mind back to the Lotus Feet every time it has moved afar, I have not spent the hour in vain. Gradually, the mind will be tranquilised and I shall taste and know how sweet it is to sit in silence.

Sitting in silence, let me repeat the Divine Name or meditate on some aspect of the Divine Reality or on an incident in the life of a man of God. God, it is true, is

Nameless: but the sages have called Him by many Names. Choose any Name that appeals to you: repeat It again and again. Repeat the Name – yes, but not merely with the tongue. Repeat It with tears in the eyes. Repeat It until you can repeat It no longer, until you disappear from yourself, your "ego" is dissolved, and you sit in the presence of the Eternal Beloved.

Abu Said was a writer of profane poetry: his poems were very popular among the lowbrows, in the Arabia of those days. One day, awakening comes to him, and renouncing the path of popularity, he goes and sits at the feet of a Teacher of spiritual life. This is what his Teacher says to him: "Abu Said! All the hundred and twenty-four thousand prophets were sent to preach one word. They bade the people, say, 'Allah,' and devote themselves to Him. Those who heard this Word by the ear alone let It go by the other ear; but those who heard It with their souls imprinted It on their souls and repeated It until It penetrated their hearts and souls, and their whole being became this Word. They were made independent of the pronunciation of the Word: they were released from the sound of the letters. Having understood the spiritual meaning of this Word, they became so absorbed in It that they were no more conscious of their own non-existence."

I sometimes think of the Name Divine as a locked door. If only we can open it, we, too, may live in the abiding presence of the Beloved. The way to open it, is the Way of Love.

We may, also, meditate on some Form of God – on Krishna or Christ, on Buddha or Nanak, on a Saint or a Holy One. God is the Formless One: but for the sake of His devotees, He has put on many Forms and visited the earth. Choose any Form that draws you: meditate on It. There should, however, be no attachment to the Form: all Forms, ultimately, have to be left behind. Significant are the words of Meister Eckhart: "He who seeks God under a settled Form lays hold of the Form, while missing the God concealed in it." Meditate on the Form to which you feel drawn – and then go beyond it. Enter into the Form to meet the Formless One!"

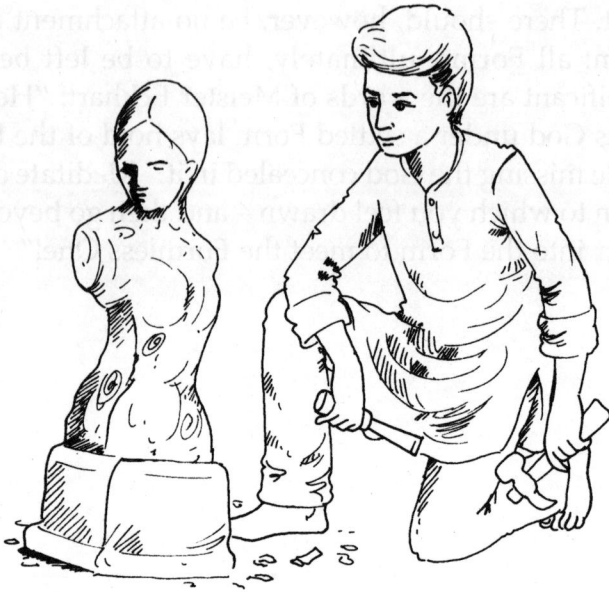

No great work has ever been produced except after a long interval of still and musing meditation.

Walter Bagehot

The life of meditation must be blended with the life of work. For we must not give up our worldly duties and obligations in order to meditate.

J. P. V.

Meditation And The Life Of Work

The life of meditation must be blended with the life of work. For we must not give up our worldly duties and obligations in order to meditate. We must withdraw ourselves from the world for a while and give ourselves wholly to God. Then we must return to our daily work, pouring into it the energy of the Spirit. Such work will bless the world. Through such work will God Himself descend upon the earth. Work of the true type is a bridge between God and humanity. So, with one hand let us cling to His Lotus Feet and with the other attend to our daily duties.

The problem, then, is how do I remember God even in the midst of multifarious activities? If, while praying we can think of worldly matters, why can we not, while doing worldly work, think of God?

- *Be Still!* From time to time, as often as I can, in the midst of daily work, of tumult and tempest, let me pause for a brief moment and lift up my heart in loving converse with God. Let me speak to Him as I speak to my dear mother or to a loving friend. My words must not have been carefully prepared, nor should they necessarily be quotations from the Scriptures. What I speak to God must flow naturally and spontaneously out of the purity and simplicity of my heart.

One day, as Sadhu Vaswani lay on his bed of sickness, there were the following words on his lips:

My heart, O Lord, is thirsty for Thy Light and Thy Love!

Come to me each day, in my thoughts and aspirations.

Come to me in my dreams, in the laughter on my lips, in the tears in my eyes.

In my worship and my work, in life and in death, come Thou to me.

Be Thou with me in Thy Mercy and Thy Love!

In moments of trial and temptation, let me call out to God, "Help me, O, Helper of the helpless ones!" Even when my foot has slipped, let me hold out my arms and cry, "Lord, lift me up!" While attending to my common duties, let me ask God to be by me, to be with me, so that every little act may become a communion with Him who hath no need of words but who is only too eager to accept the offering of love.

Bring the heart back to the sweet, familiar presence of God. Be still and let the Peace of God flow into you! It is only when the soul is at peace that true work is done, and the body and mind have the strength to bear and endure.

- *Be Calm!* Let me do nothing that may disturb my peace of mind and heart. Let my daily life be so regulated as to strengthen the inner calm, not take away from it. So let me avoid overwork. And let me not be in a hurry to do anything. Let me go about my work quietly, gently and lovingly, my mind and heart devoted to the Lotus Feet of the Lord. Then will my soul become strong and all around me the world will smile.

- *Seek God!* In the midst of my work – aye, even in the midst of my *kirtan* and worship – let me, again and again, withdraw for a brief while into the inner chamber of my heart and there speak to God, gaze upon His Beauteous Face. Let me do this from time to time throughout the day and night. Truly blessed are these brief moments of intimate contact with God, when I penetrate into the very depths of my soul and offer all I have and all I am to Him and feel grateful to Him for His everlasting mercy and loving tenderness.

This may not be accomplished within a day, a week, or a month. But nothing is impossible to him who, in faith and devotion, treads the Way of *abhyasa*, the Path of Practice. Does not the Lord declare in the Gita:

> However difficult or impossible it may seem,
> You, O Arjuna, may still achieve it,
> By steadfast effort and wholehearted devotion.
> So, walk the Way of Practice!

And as the Chinese say: "The journey of a thousand miles begins with one step." We may be far, very far, very far, from the goal. But even if we have taken a single step in the right direction, we have advanced on the Path. And for every single step that we take to reach God, God takes a hundred steps to draw nearer to us. For, while we think we are seeking God, in reality it is God who is in search of us.

No matter what technique you follow, do it right, and with one pointed mind, attention, interest and love.

Remez Sasson

All meditation techniques have the same goal – to help you achieve inner peace, tranquillity and harmony.

J. P. V.

Which Is The Right Way To Meditate?

Meditation has now become such a widely accepted practice that thousands of books have been written upon it; hundreds of techniques are propagated. It is therefore, natural for the beginner to be a little intimidated, even confused, about the 'right way' to meditate. Just as many rivers flow into the ocean, just as several paths lead up to the mountain top, so also, there may be a wide variety of practices and techniques of meditation. But the reassuring fact is that all meditation techniques have the same goal – to help you achieve inner peace, tranquility and harmony. Any method that helps you achieve this is valid.

I feel sad to hear people comparing different meditation techniques and different 'schools' of *dhyana* and arguing about which is superior to the other. A genuine teacher is aware that there is a certain universality about all meditation practices. Therefore, he will not tout superiority over the rest, nor will he encourage a 'cult' or a brand to be built around his 'school' of meditation.

Sadly, again, many aspirants fall for publicity campaigns and promotions, and even move from one meditation class to another, trying one path after another, desperate to reach their goal. Valuable time and energy are frittered away in this process – not to speak of money. After all the jumping and crossing over, people are left unhappy and frustrated because the 'goal' eludes them. Some of them even give up in despair.

Enlightened *gurus* will explain to you that no method is right or wrong, superior or inferior; as long as it helps you focus your attention within, and discover the inner dimensions of your own being. Ultimately, meditation is a matter of inner discovery, innate spirituality.

Unfortunately, neither our society nor our education really teaches us to cultivate the mind. We are taught how to observe the world outside, how to analyse external conditions and situations and how to arrive at solutions to *outer* problems. We also learn to socialise and to establish relationships with others – while we really do not know ourselves in depth!

Truly has it been said, "The whole of the body is in the mind but the whole of the mind is not in the body." If we wish to enter the mind and understand ourselves fully, meditation is the best way.

My advice to the beginner therefore, is to select a technique that appeals to you – one which suits you. Practise it regularly and consistently everyday, and at the same time everyday. You will begin to discover the benefits of meditation only after sustained and systematic practice. Meditate regularly, and you will surely succeed in your aspiration. Practice makes perfect, so continue to meditate!

"Purity, patience and perseverance," Swami Vivekananda, tells us, "these alone can lead you to success." This is especially true for aspirants on the path of *abhyasa*. Repeated and methodical practice is vital to quieten the mind and focus it inward.

There are practitioners who claim that religion has nothing to do with meditation. That is as it may be, but faith, love, prayer and God-consciousness have everything to do with meaningful meditation which is not merely an exercise like a mental fitness regime. The element of *bhakti* or devotion adds a truly spiritual dimension to the practice of meditation.

The gift of learning to
meditate is the greatest gift
you can give yourself in this
life. For it is only through
meditation that you can undertake
the journey and discover your true
nature, and so find the stability and
confidence you will need to live and
die well.

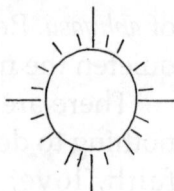

Meditation is the road to
enlightenment.

Sogyal Rinpoche

The mind needs to be cleansed of
the clutter of accumulated negative
thoughts and pressures. Meditation
empties the mind and energises the
nervous system.

Life without meditation is empty as
the desert-sands. It is very much like
a well without water, a garden
without flowers, a temple without a
light.

J. P. V.

Why Should You Meditate?

As we have seen earlier, meditation is the art of quietening, calming the mind so that our inner consciousness is stilled and becomes more aware. In the state of detachment that ensues, the practitioner attains to a higher level of consciousness.

There are several reasons why meditation is essential to the seeker in the modern context:

- The unbearable stress and strain of contemporary life needs to be countered with conscious stress-reduction techniques. Meditation is the most effective among them.
- The mind needs to be cleansed of the clutter of accumulated negative thoughts and pressures. Meditation empties the mind and energises the nervous system.
- Meditation strengthens our creativity and inner sense of harmony.
- It increases what the Zen Masters call "mindfulness" – awareness of the *here-and-the now* – so that we get the best out of ourselves and our life, every moment.
- Meditation enhances our powers of love and forgiveness and understanding.
- It makes peace and calmness, the natural condition of our minds.

- It teaches us to stop looking *outward* for our wants, needs and desires; it focuses our attention *inward*, where lasting peace and joy are to be found.
- It is the best known cure for restlessness and fragmented thinking.
- It brings steadiness to our mind, improving our powers of concentration and memory.
- It helps us avoid the two extreme states of single-minded obsession (monomania) and multi-minded distraction, both of which disturb the mind, thus closing many avenues of insight and wisdom that will be available to us.
- It stabilizes the senses and teaches the value of introversion.
- It educates us to become tolerant, patient, understanding and sympathetic individuals.
- As we evolve on the path of *abhyasa*, meditation opens possibilities of vital spiritual experiences. These are not just confined to out-of-body, or floating experiences, but deeply intuitive experiences that make us aware of the higher dimensions of life, leading us on to the highest reality.

A beginner needs a quiet place to meditate. Someone with a lot of practice can meditate everywhere and under all circumstances.

Remez Sasson

All you need is devotion to God and the guru, determination to follow the chosen path and the perseverance and patience to adhere to your discipline.

J. P. V.

Preparing To Meditate: Where And When?

The Right Place:

Our *rishis, munis* and spiritual seekers turned their back on society; they left the cities, towns and villages, gave up the company of their fellow human beings and went to the deep forests, hidden caves, isolated vales or remote peaks to practise their austerities. Solitude, isolation and a natural, serene environment helped them to focus and concentrate their attention inward.

Even now, when the devout gather together for their spiritual retreats, such an environment of solitude and natural beauty is chosen, so that it may be condusive to serenity and tranquility of mind. Necessities are provided to them to meet their minimum requirements, so that they can devote their attention to higher matters.

But what of the aspirant, the beginner on the path who is not a renunciate or an ascetic? One can hardly retire to scenic locations and remote valleys or sacred rivers to seek peace and solitude!

We are also apt to imagine that wealthy people who live in palatial mansions can easily find the appropriate place for meditation – an exclusive, separate room with all material facilities to help them concentrate….ah, what

76

would we not give for such luxurious, serene surroundings?

Does this mean that those of us who live in humbler dwellings with other family members, cannot meditate in peace?

Certainly not!

While it is true that peace, solitude and isolation are condusive to meditation, let me also add that *location* is secondary to the determined aspirant. The limitations of the simplest, ordinary, middle class home can be transcended by choosing one's favourite silence-corner, creating holy vibrations by remembering God and the Guru and retiring into one's own soul, *simply ignoring* external noises and disturbances.

Do you know that there are commuters on Mumbai locals whose only opportunity for meditation is on the crowded trains in which they travel to and fro everyday?

I am not suggesting that you should climb into a local train to meditate. All I am suggesting is that space should not be a constraint for the seeker.

Prema has taken on the practise of *abhyasa*. She lives in a hostel room with three other girls. She wakes up at five every morning, an hour before her friends are ready to get up, and sits quietly on her bed, practising her meditation.

The determination to follow the path of *abhyasa* is essential; love for meditation is enough to turn the mind inward; outer things will not disturb the seeker.

If you have the space and the facilities, you may light a lamp or a candle before the image of your *ishta devta* or *Gurudeva*; you may also use incense or *agarbattis* to create an atmosphere of fragrance; some people also like soothing, healing music to be played. All this will create the right ambience for meditation.

If possible, reserve a small corner of your home as a silence-corner, to be set aside for meditation, silent prayer or *naam-japa*. Any corner will do – provided it is clean, quiet and well-ventilated. A dark, musty or stuffy corner will make it uncomfortable for you to concentrate. Too much noise or exposure will also disturb your concentration. It is best that this corner should be as away as possible from the television and the telephone.

Many teachers recommend that you should sit comfortably on a mat or folded sheet or a cushion, so that you are not disturbed by physical discomforts like a cold floor, or a hard surface. Some experts even tell you to avoid the bare floor – for it may absorb the spiritual energy generated through meditation.

However, these are not the essentials of meditation. All you need is this: devotion to God and the *guru*, determination to follow the chosen path and the perseverance and patience to adhere to your discipline. The rest does not really matter.

The Right Time:

We saw earlier, that 'time' is a great constraint for a few aspirants. However, this is a factor that cannot be compromised. Regularity of practice is essential for successful, meaningful, purposeful meditation. The aspirant must cultivate the quality of efficient time-management and make it a point to devote a regular 'slot' for his *abhyasa*.

If you cannot find the time to meditate regularly, you will not succeed!

78

Let me add, it is possible for all of us to work out a daily schedule, a time-table that will help you to find a convenient time and place for your daily practise.

In a spiritual retreat, the aspirant should find the opportunity to devote two or three 'sittings' everyday for the purpose of meditation. As for those of us who live in our worldly environment, we should find time to devote atleast 30 minutes to our meditation everyday.

Most experts will tell you that you can meditate whenever you find time – morning, noon or evening. However, I must add that certain time-periods have been found to be best suited for *abhyasa*: early mornings or late evenings, the *daivik* (divine) hours of dawn and twilight, when an atmosphere of serenity and quietness prevails. Such times have their influence also, on the mind of the seeker; they condition his internal state, making successful meditation possible.

For mothers with young children, it is recommended that they should devote such periods of time when the children do not need their attention – i.e. when the children are asleep, or playing outside the house.

You must choose a time when you will be able to focus on your meditation without disturbing others, and without undue inconvenience to yourself. You must not feel pre-occupied with tasks waiting to be completed; you must not feel guilty about duties being ignored. This is why it is recommended that one should rise early in the morning to meditate – before the daily 'rush' begins.

There are some people who feel particularly alert, alive and energetic at certain times of the day; at other times, their 'body clock' seems to slow down, and they do not feel up to much activity – mental or physical. All of us must become familiar with our own bio-rhythm, as it is called, so that we may choose the time that suits us best.

For many people, the quiet hours of the dawn or the last half an hour before one retires to bed, are the preferred slots for meditation. Each of us must choose a time-slot depending on our own schedule and commitments.

It is important to meditate everyday without fail for at least 15-20 minutes, at first. Beginners are often told to meditate *twice* daily, so that they get into the routine comfortably. *Regularity* is very essential for the aspirant.

I know some executives who 'switch off' to meditate for a few minutes just before lunch or at the end of a hectic working day. This helps to break the tension, stress and hassle of the work; it breaks the cycle of pressure and strain, and helps to "centre" you for the rest of the day.

I also know nurses and doctors who meditate briefly during their breaks. This helps them to stay calm, focussed and in-control during emergencies.

You will make excellent progress on the path of *abhyasa* by setting aside a regular time and following a regular schedule for meditation. When this becomes a fixed habit, a definite part of your daily routine, it will help you to advance further on the path.

If your schedule does not permit you to find such a fixed slot, try to find one or two alternative slots which will help you to establish some sort of regularity. This will overcome initial mental resistance and the general human tendency to put off for tomorrow what must be done everyday!

The ancient scriptures tell us that four 'auspicious' hours of the day and night are particularly suited for meditation:

1) The sacred hour prior to the dawn – the *brahma muhurat* or hour of the gods as it is called.
2) The hour of the noon – when everything is hushed and nature seems to be still. Even birds and insects are quiet – and people at home are resting.
3) Early evening – when lamps are lit, the sun sinks down in the western horizon and the earth and the sky assume a different colour, a different light, a different *aura*.
4) The midnight hour – when the world is asleep; and even the moon and the stars watch over us in quiet and stillness. Many people believe that midnight is the most peaceful time for meditation.

I have a personal preference for the early morning hour, and I have no hesitation in recommending it to you, too. The mind is quiet, peaceful, refreshed and rested after the night's sleep; all the negative impressions accumulated on the previous day have been erased; and you have a fresh, clean, blank page on which to begin writing. Above all, when you begin the day with God and meditate before you start your daily routine, you will not only find yourself spiritually and emotionally energised; you will also get a positive direction and power, to take you through the rest of the day.

Practical Suggestions

- Some people find it easier to meditate after a shower or a bath. Pious *brahmins* perform the *sandhyavandana* regularly after their bath – and this includes the

81

practice of *pranayama* and the recital of the *Gayatri Mantra*. This is obviously because cleanliness of the body is associated with purification of the inner instrument.

If you are unable to have a shower or bath, you can wash your face, hands and feet before you sit down to meditate.

- You should wear clean, light, comfortable clothes that are not too tight or restrictive.
- It is not recommended to start your meditation after a large meal.

When you have just eaten a main meal, the body systems are focused on the process of digestion. The subtle nerves of the body become heavy and your consciousness will not be alert and awake – nor at its best.

Many experts suggest meditating on an empty stomach. But then again, hunger will hinder your concentration. The ideal time would be *atleast two hours* after a meal. Obviously, an early morning meditation will nullify these problems.

- If a disturbing, noisy environment prevails, it is best to postpone your meditation. Instead, you can read a holy book, recite a prayer or do *naam-japa*.
- Some aspirants find it refreshing and vitalising to meditate occasionally, in the midst of nature. But this cannot be done on a daily, regular basis. For 'meditation' is really a process of 'interiorization'. Swami Paramahansa Yoganand called this "shutting off the sense telephones." Our ancient sages called this stage *pratyahara* – gathering the scattered forces of the mind.

Posture:

Let me begin by telling you – meditation is a simple technique that all of us can and must practise. This book is not a manual of hard-and-fast rules and regulations for meditation.

Therefore, this is my first word to you regarding posture: all you need to do is to sit quietly, comfortably, in a relaxed and steady position.

Still, steady, relaxed and comfortable: this is essential. Complicated, cross-legged positions which you cannot even form with your limbs, leave alone being comfortable, are not really necessary. The "lotus pose" may not come easily to you, or the Chinese method of sitting on your lower legs.

There is only one important requisite for a good meditation posture – and this is stressed by every expert without exception – the head, neck and trunk of the body should be aligned in a straight line so that you breathe freely and effortlessly – using your diaphragm, and not merely your chest.

The spine should be kept straight and erect. The head and neck should be centred – that is, the neck should not be twisted, or the head held forward. The head should be supported firmly by the neck and held directly over the shoulders, without creating any tension in the muscles. The facial region should be completely relaxed, paying special attention to ensure that there is no tension in the region of the jaw. Your arms should be relaxed and allowed to rest gently on the knees – in such a way that if someone were to pick up your hand, your arm will be limp. The thumb and the index finger can touch gently so as also to form a circle, while the rest of the fingers should be held straight. This posture, it is said, recycles the energy you generate *within* you, instead of allowing it to escape.

Many Indians as well as Japanese, Vietnamese and Chinese people find it quite comfortable to sit on the floor. But if you find it difficult, or if you have problems with your back-muscles, you may even sit on a straight backed chair – holding your spine straight.

You can choose a chair with a padded seat and a straight back. Do no lean against the back of the chair, for this brings pressure upon your spine. Keep your shoulders a little back so that they don't slump. And I repeat, a straight spine is essential. If you slump, muscles acquire tension in order to support your weight and a bent spine also inhibits the flow of subtle energies.

Practical Suggestions:

- It is recommended that you sit on a woollen blanket or a folded sheet, to block magnetic forces of the earth.
- Experts say that the arms and legs are not really crucial in the meditation posture. It is enough if your legs are not twisted in an uncomfortable manner.
- The *Sukhasana* or comfortable posture is recommended for beginners. It is a simple, cross-legged position, with your feet placed on the floor under the knees, while the knees rest gently on them. It is advisable to face east, and sit on the edge of a cushion so that the coccyx rests on the cushion.
- Physical exercises or *Hatha Yoga* will help you acquire a relaxed body and flexible muscles. Stretching exercises in particular will help you make your body comfortable in your chosen meditation posture.

- It is not recommended to meditate in a lying position. First and foremost, you are likely to fall asleep. Even if you don't, you will not be fully alert and awake when you are lying down – and alertness is vital in meditation.
- Sitting on a folded blanket or a cushion relieves pressure on the hip joints and knees. Be patient while you develop a sitting posture that is comfortable to you. As your body becomes more flexible, you will find that you will be able to sit for larger periods without feeling any discomfort.
- There are several sitting postures that can be used equally effectively. What matters most is that you should be comfortable and your spine should be straight.
- Experts also give a subtle reason why the spine should be held straight: only when it is correctly aligned will energy move upward through the body.
- Remember, above all, that whatever posture you may choose, your mind should be fixed on God – not on the pain in your knees, the tension in your shoulder or the constriction in your neck.

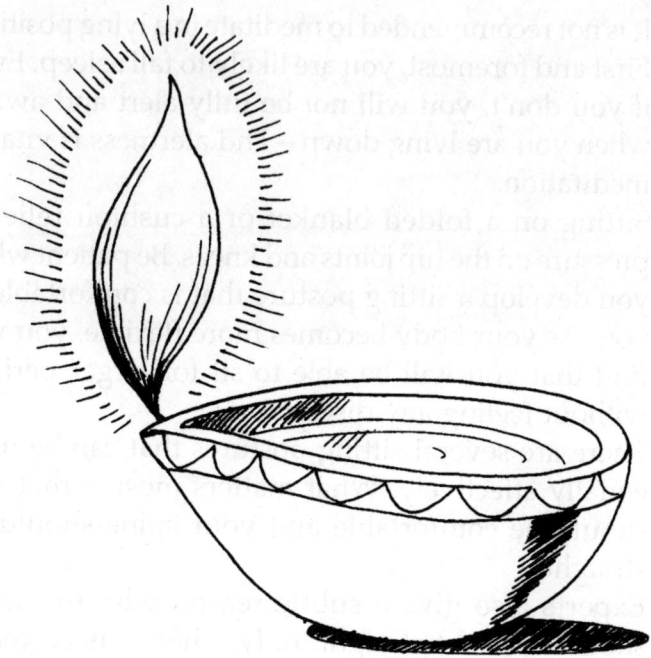

When meditation is mastered, the
mind is unwavering like the flame of
a lamp in a windless place.

Bhagavad Gita

The mark of a perfect man is this —
that he wanders not. The perfect
man is one whose wandering has
ceased.

J. P. V.

Quietening The Mind

Now, you are seated in a comfortable, relaxed posture, spine erect, head, neck and trunk aligned in a straight line.

The question now arises: *what do I do?*

Should I try to *think* certain thoughts; should I *empty* the mind of all *thoughts* or simply let the mind *drift*, with its own memories and associations flowing in.

Let me reiterate: meditation is not the same as *thinking* or *reflection*. Some experts even assert that meditation begins where thinking ends. In order to meditate, we must put aside our tendency to 'think out' issues, seek solutions to problems and difficulties, plan for the future, react to circumstances or to judge people and situations. In short, we must learn to *let go* – let go of problems and worries, let go of our ego, let go of our past and future.

Meditation is not allowing the mind to drift either: when the mind drifts, it indulges in fantasies and daydreams. Meditation, it is said, should help you rise above both the dreamy subconscious and the restless conscious mind. The aim of meditation, as I have already said, is to bring us in touch with our Superconscious State.

This involves three stages, as experts point out to us: relaxation, interiorization and expansion. Let me explain the process in stages:

1) You become utterly relaxed in body and mind.
2) You focus your attention, you concentrate single-mindedly on the object of your meditation.
3) As a culmination of this process of concentration, you expand your own sense of identity, until you realise your unity with all creation, the entire universe, and with the One who pervades all creation and the entire universe.

Meditation, as I said, is a journey within – and this journey can begin only when you withdraw your attention from the exterior world. For this, you need to be entirely relaxed; and you need to concentrate.

- Do not try to strive or achieve anything. Do not attempt to 'make' anything happen in the mind. This only brings frustration.
- Do not attempt to 'control' the mind either; your mind will only fight such an attempt.
- The less you 'strive' or 'fight', the more relaxed you will feel – and achieve the beautiful stillness that is essential in meditation.
- 'Emptying' the mind will not work either. Rather, attempt to quieten or still the mind – by giving it one focus.
- Remember – concentration is not analysis or reasoning. It does not involve any kind of stress or tension – as it happens, when we are concentrating on a 'problem' or even a text or a lecture or a task that we are trying to accomplish. The concentration of meditation involves no strain or pressure – it is a

process of focussing our attention, as opposed to a scattered, wandering, distracted state of mind. This kind of concentration is a prelude to meditation.

Life is a pilgrimage. March towards the goal. And remember your goal is God.

Sadhu Vaswani

The secret of success of meditation is – grace of Guru and God.

Look forward to the hour of meditation with deep love and longing of the heart and also keep on begging for God's grace to be poured on your efforts.

J. P. V.

How Do I Proceed?

The following are only a few "guidelines" and need not be strictly adhered to. Meditation is a most 'personal' experience in which one's deepest and truest self is involved.

Every person meditates in his or her way, for the "Spirit bloweth where it listeth". The one who treads the path of meditation becomes a pilgrim of the Spirit, always on the move, always eager to sink deeper and deeper within himself, until he loses himself in the Pure White Light. The following, therefore, are only a few practical suggestions:

1. Select a silence-corner of a silence-chamber where you can spend some time everyday without being disturbed. It should preferably be away from the telephone and should be dimly lighted.

2. It is advisable to get up as early as possible in the morning – in any case, before sunrise. The period of three hours before sunrise is known as *brahma muhurat*, and is especially favourable for meditation. At that time, the atmosphere is calm and serene, the body is fresh and rested, the mind is alert but not overactive. The hour of evening twilight is also good for meditation.

   If, however, these hours are not found convenient, any other suitable time may be fixed.

91

3. If, at the time of meditation, you feel drowsy, there is no harm if you have a cup of tea or coffee or if you walk up and down for sometime or do a light exercise.

4. Meditation should be practised preferably at the same time and at the same place, everyday. This will help form a habit that will automatically throw you into a meditative mood when the hour approaches.

5. Meditation should be practised when the body is not tired and at least two hours after having a meal.

6. At the time of meditation, it is helpful to wear loose comfortable clothes. This will help you to relax fully. The clothes should be clean and, if possible, set apart for this purpose.

7. No particular posture is prescribed for meditation. Adopt any sitting posture that you find natural and in which you can sit steadily for some length of time without having to move the body unnecessarily. You may sit on the floor (not on the bare ground but on a mat, a carpet or a piece of cloth) in a cross-legged position or be seated in a straight chair with your feet gently resting on the floor. What is important is that the spinal column and the head should be held erect. This helps the *prana* (vital energy) to move freely in the body. Do not strain. Be comfortable, relaxed and attentive.

8. If, in the course of meditation, you feel cramps or pain or get an itching sensation in any part of the body, do not move but concentrate on the part where you feel the pain (or itch or any other sensation) and mentally repeat the word *pain...pain...pain...*(or *itch...itch...itch* and so on) over and over again; the pain will disappear and you can continue your practice of meditation.

92

9. It helps to wear a soft smile on the face. This aids in brightening the mind and makes it happier.
10. Relax. Take a few deep breaths. Also, take God's Name a few times in such a way that its resonance is mentally heard. Turn the mind either inward or upward. There are three centres in which you may fix the attention of the mind: (a) the heart (not the physical heart but what is called the "spiritual heart" – it is in the middle of the chest, in line with the physical heart); (b) the point between (and a little behind) the two eyebrows; and (c) the crown of the head. Choose the centre where the consciousness easily and naturally settles down.
11. You do not have to concentrate or meditate upon these positions. You have only to station yourself in your consciousness at one of these centres and be there for the duration of the meditation.
12. As you try to concentrate, you will find that, in the early stages, untoward thoughts will make your attention wander; this is natural. The mind has the habit of wandering: it must wander. You will be annoyed at how many and how trivial these distractions can be. You must deal with them kindly. Do not drive them out in anger. Be gentle with them. Label each distraction as past-present-future-worthy-unworthy-jealousy-envy-hatred-vanity-desire-egoism, and so on. As you label them, they will slink away and leave you in peace. Once they disappear, your attention will return to meditation.
13. If, during the meditation, you see any lights or figures or images (or hear sounds or notice a fragrance), observe them in a detached manner. Do not feel elated: do not shut them out. They are

generally signs of the opening of the subtler senses of sight or sound or smell. Some people have such experiences: others do not. Experiences, by themselves, may mean nothing. What is important is attaining to purity, peace, love, compassion, joy. What is important is the transformation of one's life.

14. After meditation, do not immediately plunge into active work. Be quiet for some time and gently move out of the world of silence into the world of activity.

15. You must carry the spirit of meditation into the workaday world. The peace and purity you have experienced in periods of silence must be reflected in your dealings with others. Emotions like hatred, anger, resentment, ill-will, greed, arrogance, self-love, covetousness, envy, jealousy, agitation and anxiety must be transcended.

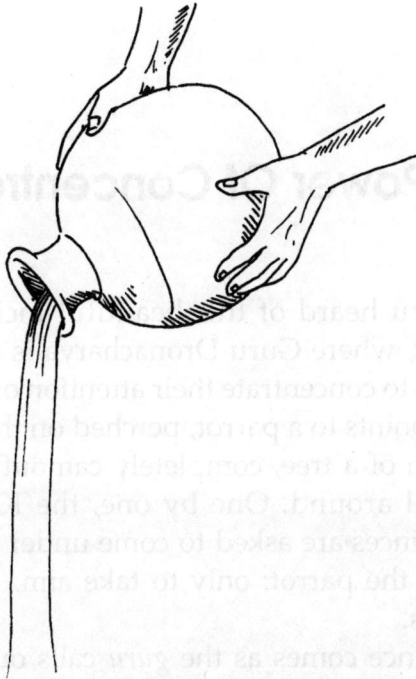

In deep meditation the flow of concentration is continuous like the flow of oil.

Patanjali

Concentration is the ability to focus vision, thought and mind in a unified function.

J. P. V.

The Power Of Concentration

Have you heard of this beautiful incident in the *Mahabharata*, where Guru Dronacharya is teaching his royal pupils to concentrate their attention on the chosen target? He points to a parrot, perched on the green and leafy branch of a tree, completely camouflaged in the greenery all around. One by one, the Kaurava and Pandava princes are asked to come under the tree and take aim at the parrot: only to take aim, *not* to shoot their arrows.

Each prince comes as the *guru* calls out his name. Each strings his bow, fixes his arrow and takes aim.

"What do you see?" asks the *guru* of each one, as he stands beneath the tree and looks up at the bird.

"I can see the green leaves fluttering in the wind," one replies.

"The glare of the sunlight through the leaves almost blinds me," says another.

And so they come and go; one can hardly see the parrot for the leaves; another sees glimpses of the blue sky *above*; one complains that the bird is barely visible.

"I can see its sharp, brown claws and its pointed, red beak clearly!" exclaims Duryodhana. "I see the bird clearly!"

The last to take aim is Arjuna, the *guru's* favourite disciple. He too, comes and takes aim, looking up steadily, directly.

"What do you see?" the *guru* asks again.

"I see only the eye of the parrot," Arjuna replies.

"What else do you see?" the *guru* asks. "Can you see the leaves, the sunlight trickling through the leaves from the blue sky beyond?"

"I can see none of these," replies Arjuna. "I can only see the eye of the parrot."

This is concentration – the ability to focus vision, thought and mind in a unified function.

The Chinese sage Chuang Tzu relates an interesting story. There was a man who used to forge swords for the Minister of War. He was eighty years old – and yet his work was perfect. He never once slipped.

The Minister of War once asked him, "Is it just your inborn ability, the skill you have acquired or is it the method you follow?"

"It is none of these," the old man replied. "It is just concentration. I started forging swords when I was twenty years old. I cared for nothing else. If a thing were not a sword, I simply did not notice it. I just gave all my energy and effort and attention to making swords."

Concentration has been defined by a wise teacher as wholeness, unity and equilibrium – a unification of the senses and the faculties. They must work in unified harmony.

Meditation is not possible without concentration. And I don't just mean lower levels of concentration such as we use at work or in the laboratory. I mean the kind of higher concentration in which the mind gathers its full strength through singleness, becoming steadfast and focussed, attaining union with the One. This is what Socrates refers to when he says:

Thought is best when the mind is gathered into herself and is aspiring after true being.

The practice of unified, single-minded focus on one subject, is concentration. When it is turned inward, it becomes meditation. As Sri Krishna tells us in the *Bhagavad Gita*:

> As a lamp placed in a windless spot does not flicker, nor does a *yogi* of subdued mind practising union with the self.

When the mind becomes truly focused, we enter into a new dimension of consciousness. "Seeing Self by the Self, we are satisfied in the Self alone." When our mind touches the Supreme, it kindles the inner flame and we become illumined souls. For, as the philosopher Plotinus says:

> ... it is not possible to see Him or be in harmony with Him while one is occupied with anything else. The soul must remove from itself everything, that it may receive the One alone, as the One is alone.

This oneness with the One, is what we hope to achieve through meditation.

Meditate daily, and soon your inner strength and mind power will grow.

Remez Sasson

Some people think that meditation takes time away from physical accomplishment. Taken to extremes, of course, that's true. Most people, however, find that meditation creates more time than it takes.

J. P. V.

How Long Should You Meditate?

Many people force themselves to sit through hour-long meditation sessions, sometimes twice or thrice a day. They try to ignore acute physical discomfort and desperately fight to control their wandering minds – all because they feel that repeated, extended attempts at meditation are good for them.

This is as unnecessary as it is unprofitable. To force oneself, push oneself beyond one's capacity is surely counter-productive. At times, even a quick but concentrated five-minute meditation may be more effective than hours of forced *abhyasa* – provided for those five minutes, you devote all your attention and effort to your meditation.

It is vital that meditation should be undertaken with enthusiasm and sincerity. If you are troubled by the rigour and ardour of the process of meditation it cannot bring you any benefit. In fact, I would even urge beginners – when you begin to feel discomfort or distraction, you must give up the attempt to meditate, and begin again when you are calm and relaxed.

Meditation must become a deeply relaxing exercise to which you return regularly, with energy and enthusiasm. It must not become a dreaded chore which you take up mechanically.

Beginners can start with fifteen-minutes sessions, so that the mind is able to quieten and calm down. As you get used to sitting still and emptying the mind, you can gradually increase the period of meditation, taking it up to half an hour or more – depending on your schedule.

It would be good to meditate at least *twice* a day, with half an hour for each session, preferably before the day begins and before you retire to bed.

In this as in many other things, regularity is essential. It is better to meditate for at least a few minutes everyday, rather than force oneself through hour-long sessions for a week – and then give up in frustration.

Once again, let me quote Paramhansa Yogananda: "The more you meditate, the more you will want to meditate. But the less you meditate, the less you will want to meditate."

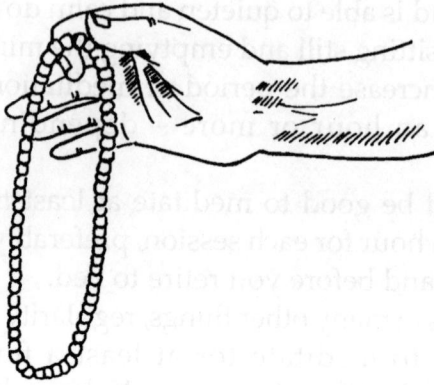

Constant repetition of the *Ram Mantra* and the practise of meditation will give you the needed strength and courage to overcome all weaknesses of the mind and the heart.

Swami Ramdas

N aam smaran, mantra japa and *dhyana* are at the very foundation of *abhyasa*. Together, they quieten the agitated mind, cleanse the mind of all its impurities, leaving us calm and serene to enter into meditation.

J. P. V.

The Value Of *Mantra*

In its strictest form, a *mantra* is not an expression with meaning; it is a sound, a *shabda* with its own special and unique vibrations. Of course, when we utter the sacred Name aloud, the sounds create their own waves. But when they vibrate in silence, within us, they have a tremendously beneficial effect on our being. In fact, according to the Hindu tradition, our ancient sages who sat in deep meditation for a lifetime, heard these sounds in the silence within their souls; the sounds they heard – *shruti* - have now become the *mantras* which we use.

Nowadays, we attach meaning and value only to that which is uttered in words: silence, and the eloquence of silence is lost on most of us. Therefore, it requires practice to appreciate and absorb the vibrations that a *mantra* produces at a much deeper level than words. Rather than look for any *meaning*, we must learn to *experience* the vibrations at a profound level.

A whole book could be written on the fascinating subject of the inter-relation of *mantra* and meditation. Suffice it to say that *mantras* heard within, produce healing, soothing vibrations, so that we attain a level of experience that is deeper than mere thought.

The repetition of the *mantra* bestowed on you by your *guru* has great power and efficacy; not only does it strengthen your faith and devotion, but it also purifies your mind, heart and soul. Our saints and sages tell us that *naam smaran* can absolve us of all sins and lead us on to salvation – but this is possible only when the *mantra* is uttered with perfect faith and reverence; and the *mantra* that is heard in the heart within is far more efficacious than one that is uttered aloud.

Concentrate on a *mantra*, a Holy Name, a Word or Syllable, which to you is symbolic of God or Truth (the shorter the *mantra*, the better). Repeat It again and again. Repeat It in a musical manner. Repeat It with deep love and longing of the heart. Repeat It until It gets fixed in your mind and is in the background of your consciousness all the time – even while you are working or are asleep.

Any *mantra* or Holy Name or Word or Syllable that draws you may be taken up. God is the Nameless One: the sages have called Him by many Names. All Names will lead you to the Nameless One. There is the ancient *mantra*, "Om" or "Raam". There is the *maha-mantra*, "Hare Raam, Hare Raam, Raam, Raam, Hare, Hare; Hare Krishna, Hare Krishna, Krishna, Krishna, Hare, Hare." There are other *mantras:* "Om Namoh Bhagavate Vaasudevaaya", "Om Namah Shivaaya", "Om Sri Raam, Jaya Raam, Jaya, Jaya, Raam", "Raam Krishna Hari", "Satnaam", "Waahguru", "Om Mani Padme Hum", "Jesus", "Lord Jesus Christ, have mercy on me", "Jehovaah", "Allah", "Ahura Mazda". The list is endless.

Many meditative traditions use *mantras*. But we would do well to remember, that these should be heard from *within*, not from the outside.

There was a pious young man who served his *guru* with great faith and devotion. When the *guru* felt he was evolved enough to tread the spiritual path on his own, he was called to the *guru's* presence. The *guru* gave him a personal *mantra* and said to him, "This is a secret which is known to very few, that I have bestowed on you. Please recite it in the heart within. Take care that you do not divulge it to anyone – for it is very precious."

The disciple began to practise the *mantra japa* with great sincerity and reverence. It became almost a part of his breathing – as he recited it silently.

One day, as he was returning after a sacred dip in the river, he passed by a few men who had just taken their bath. To his utter amazement he heard them uttering the same *mantra* aloud, as they smeared holy ash on their forehead, and prepared to commence their morning rituals.

"How can this be?" the disciple thought to himself. "My Master told me to guard the secret *mantra* with my life – and these men are repeating it aloud as if it is a part of their routine? Could I have been mistaken...?"

When doubt enters the heart, who but the *guru* can resolve it?

He went straight to his Master and placed his problem at the holy one's feet.

The Master heard him out patiently. Then he took a sizeable glassy stone from his pouch and gave it to the disciple.

"Take it to the *bazaar* and show it to people you know," the *guru* said to him. "Ask them what they think it is, and also to what use they would put it."

The disciple took the stone and said he would do as the *guru* ordered.

"Only remember, on no account must you give the stone away to any one," the *guru* added. "It must be brought back here without fail."

105

The disciple set out. The first person he met in the *bazaar* was an old woman who sold vegetables to him daily.

"Take a look at this stone, *chachi*," he said to her, showing the glassy object to her. "What do you think it is?"

The old woman took it in her hand and peered at it closely.

"Looks like a piece of white marble," she said, handing it back to him.

"What would you do with it if it were yours?" the man enquired.

"You know *beta*, I don't have a 50 gm weight for my balance," the old lady said. "I could use this stone as a substitute for the missing weight."

The man took the stone and proceeded to the shop of his friend, a moneylender. The same questions were posed to him, too. The moneylender thought that the stone was an uncut semi-precious mineral, and said that he would use it as an unusual kind of paper weight.

A little farther down was a shop frequented by the man's wife. This shop sold artificial jewellery. When the jeweller saw the stone he pronounced it to be an artificial diamond. "I would cut it up and use it to make jewels," he said.

The last stop was at the office of his cousin who was a gemmologist. The cousin took one look at the stone and said, "Who gave it to you? This is one of the largest diamonds I have seen!"

"A real diamond?" stammered the young man. "What would you do with it if it were yours?"

"It is of no use to me as it is," said the man. "People just can't afford to buy a diamond of this size. It will have to be cut, polished and sold."

The man thanked him and took the 'stone' back to the *guru*. Faithfully, he repeated what he had heard from the people he met.

"I hope your doubt is resolved now," the *guru* said to him. "The diamond is priceless in its present form – but nobody recognised this. They only thought of putting it to a limited use that their mind suggested. In the same way, the *mantra* I gave you is a priceless treasure; others misuse it because they do not know its value. You must realise its worth and guard it as a treasure."

Naam smaran, mantra japa and *dhyana* are at the very foundation of *abhyasa*. Together, they quieten the agitated mind, cleanse the mind of all its impurities, leaving us calm and serene to enter into meditation.

Practical Tips:

- The *mantra* is heard *within* – not repeated aloud, or heard externally.
- As the *mantra* is repeated within, you will find that the mind becomes quieter, less distracted. Thoughts do arise – but you can guide the mind back to its focus by concentrating on the *mantra*.
- Do not engage in a conflict with your mind – watch, observe, witness passing thoughts with detachment; allow them to pass and bring your mind back to the *mantra* gently, patiently, without stress or strain. Other reactions only drain your mental energy.
- Do not attempt to drive away or suppress thoughts. Just notice them without judgement, without intensifying them any further.
- Some *mantras* can be co-ordinated with your breathing – such as So-Hum or Ra-Am or O-M. But

not all *mantras* work thus. The goal of concentration is not to focus on the breathing process. If you do, you will only create a distraction and disrupt the breathing process.

- Remember too, *mantras* cannot simply be learnt or read from books; a qualified yoga teacher will often give his students a personal *mantra* suited to their level of experience.

- If you have not received any *mantra*, you can meditate on the *mantra* which is enshrined in the soul of India – The *Mantra*, 'Om' (also pronounced as 'Aum') or the sacred name, 'Ram'.

Prayer is when you talk to God; meditation is when you listen to God.

Diara Robinson

Remember the 'Form' and 'Formless' aspects of God are but like two sides of the same coin. Can you have 'heads' without 'tails'? So too, God with Form is the basis that will gradually lead you on to the Formless One.

J. P. V.

The Power Of The Form

Concentrate on an object or form, which to you is symbolic of God or Truth. In the initial stages, you may take up a picture (of Krishna, Rama, Siva, Buddha, Jesus, Moses, Zoroaster, Guru Nanak, Kabir, Baha'u'llah or any other Great One) and place it in front of you at eye-level. Gaze steadily at the picture and, after sometime close your eyes and fix the picture at the centre of concentration. Do this in a relaxed manner, without strain. After sometime, the mental vision will fade away. Open your eyes again and steadily gaze at the picture. Repeat the process a number of times. A stage will come when you will be able to visualize the picture wherever you are.

Our ancient sages tell us that there are two types of *dhyana: saguna* (with form) and *nirguna* (formless). Meditating on the form of your *ishta devta* or *guru* is *saguna dhyana;* meditation on the inner flame within you is *nirguna dhyana.*

Many teachers will tell you that 'gross' meditation – i.e. meditation upon a form – is not regarded so highly as 'subtle' or formless meditation. But I feel that as long as we exist on a physical plane, the form will always remain special to us – and therefore, it will do the beginner no harm to meditate upon the form of a Beloved one, in order to help him achieve concentration.

In the early stages of *abhyasa*, it is only natural that we think of the One, as a Divine Form. God with Form is a familiar image in the minds and hearts of many. We have grown to love and revere the Form of the Beloved. And a visual image always helps us to focus on thoughts when we begin to concentrate.

Non-religious practitioners or those who do not believe in a 'God' as faith-filled people do, often choose to visualise a *scene*: such as a large green meadow; or a deep golden light; or even a snow-covered, majestic mountain. These images induce calm and serenity in the mind.

However, for believers, there is nothing like the form of the God or the *guru*, to help them attune themselves with the superconscious. When you have gazed with love and longing upon the Beloved Form, close your eyes and clearly visualise the image in your mind's eye.

Internalise the Form, and then dwell on the attributes of the Beloved, until your mind is flooded with peace and bliss.

Remember, when you begin meditation upon a Form, you are not just worshipping the Form; rather you receive inspiration from the Form, and enhance your spiritual aspiration. For example, when you meditate on a lamp, or a flame, neither lamp nor flame is God; but God is on the flame and the lamp, and this helps you in your effort to achieve perfect concentration.

As you progress on the path, the Formless One will replace the Form – the object will recede, but the mind will be transformed by its initial contemplation. You will then find it possible to dwell on the Formless, Attributeless, Absolute Being. Thus there are three stages in the experience:

111

1. Meditation upon the Form.
2. Meditation on the Attributes of the Divine.
3. Meditation on the Formless – or pure consciousness.

1. Blend methods 1 and 2. Concentrate on the Form, and, at the same time, keep on repeating the Name Divine. You will find this practice very rewarding.
2. Concentrate on an incident from the life of your Master, Krishna, Buddha, Jesus, and so on. Let your mind revolve around the incident. Say to yourself (mentally), *The Master was so patient. He was so loving, forgiving…. When shall I be likewise?* Through concentration on such incidents, you will sink deeper and deeper within yourself.
3. Concentrate on a subtle object: an idea, an aspiration, a quality such as love, joy, peace, humility, compassion, tranquility…
4. Do not concentrate directly on God (the Supreme Being), but concentrate on God existing in the heart of your Guru and on whom the Guru himself is meditating with unflinching devotion and perfect concentration. The Guru may be a living person or, better still, a Great One who has passed on – a saint, a prophet, a man of God. Have a mental picture of the Guru in the act and posture of deep meditation and, as you meditate on the object of his meditation, you will be richly rewarded.
5. Concentrate on a "saying" or an "utterance" of a Great One, or a *sloka*, a line from a Scripture that is dear to you. (A few thoughts for meditation are given at the end of this book.) Repeat the words a

number of times. Let the mind revolve around the words. Enter into the depths of meaning that are contained in the words. This will produce a train of thoughts centering around the "saying" or "utterance." A stage will come when thoughts will vanish, and you will have gone beyond the "mind".

6. Concentrate on your breathing. Feel the air come in at the tip of the nostrils as you inhale. Feel the air flow out at the tip of the nostrils as you exhale. Do not follow the breath as it enters the lungs. Do not control your breathing. Do not attempt to deepen it. This is not an exercise in breathing. Do not interfere with your breathing. Only feel the air at the tip of the nostrils, as it comes in and flows out. You will find that your attention will wander, again and again. All you have to do is gently bring back your attention to the process. Do not struggle with thoughts or feelings. Gently bring back your attention to your breath. It will grow quieter and quieter. It will slow down to a point of almost indistinguishable rhythm. You must not tense your muscles. Non-effort is the key to success in meditation.

7. As you practise this meditation, you will gradually find in the words of a great teacher, that "your breathing is your greatest friend. Return to it in all your troubles and you will find comfort and guidance."

8. As you sit to meditate, turn your attention inward, observe the natural breathing cycle, and with inhalation listen to the sound of one part of a *mantra* and with exhalation listen to the other part of the *mantra*. For instance, if your *mantra* is Om Raam, with

inhalation listen to the sound of "Om", with exhalation listen to the sound of "Raam". If your *mantra* is *Soham*, with inhalation listen to the sound of "*So*", with exhalation listen to the sound of "*ham*". You do not have to utter the *mantra* mentally. You have to listen to the sound in your mind.

9. Keep a lighted candle (with a sufficiently strong flame) at eye level, say at a distance of about fifteen inches. Take a deep breath and mentally say to yourself: I am surrounded by the loving Light of the Spirit. Continue to gaze steadily at the flame for some time, keeping blinking to a minimum. Then close your eyes and pay attention to the image of the flame at the point between the two eyebrows. Gradually the image will fade away. Open your eyes and repeat the procedure (that is, gaze steadily at the flame, and so on). You may repeat this practice a few times.

There are many other methods. Choose the one you like and be regular in your practice. In the beginning, there will be days when the practice will be dry, boring, tiresome. Do not, on that account, give up the practice. New grooves are to be cut. Through a process of many births, the mind has acquired the habit of wandering. And it will take some time for this wandering to cease.

After some months of repeated and regular practice, you will arrive at a stage where you will be filled with indescribable joy and happiness. This is known as the "bliss of concentration". Those who have tasted it but once miss it greatly if perchance, some day, due to overwork or otherwise, they are unable to sit in silence.

Many, today, are turning to meditation to reduce the effects of stress and anxiety, to grow in awareness, to improve their health or emotional stability. They achieve the results they are looking for. But it must not be forgotten that the true goal of meditation is God. Meditation should aim at detaching the heart from all that is not-God, and at giving to it, as its sole occupation, communion with the Divine Being. Therefore, even in the midst of your daily work, pause for a while and breathe out an aspiration such as, "I love You, God! I want to love You more and more! I want to love You more than anything in the world! I want to love You to distraction! Grant me pure love and devotion for Your Lotus Feet, and so bless me that this world-bewitching *maya* may not lead me astray, and make me, Blessed Master, an instrument of Thy help and healing in this world of suffering and pain!"

Where there is love, meditation becomes easy and natural.

The affairs of the world will go on forever. Do not delay the practice of meditation.

Milarepa

All of us are capable of contemplation and introspection. We have only to take the first step.

J. P. V.

Meditation For All

An erroneous notion prevails among people, that meditation is meant only for ascetics, renunciates or those who are not leading "wordly" lives.

Let me assure you, the path of *abhyasa*, the path of self-realisation, the path of spiritual well-being, is open to one and all.

Our ancient sages classified the goals of life as four-fold: *artha* (wealth); *kama* (desire); *dharma* (religion); and *moksha* (liberation). Those of us who strive for the first two, may be described as worldly seekers. But beyond a certain point, these objectives fail to give us true satisfaction. It is only then that we turn to the spiritual path.

Meditation enables even the worldly seeker to tread the spiritual path. Even while we are in the world and of it, we are not dragged downward, but learn to dwell on our spiritual upliftment and advancement. After all, liberation is the goal that all of us seek.

All of us are capable of contemplation and introspection. Alas, very few systems of education train us in this direction. Therefore, we require self-discipline and self-motivation to tread the path of *abhyasa*.

Expectant mothers must learn to meditate, so that their unborn children may receive the vital vibrations and energies generated from them. It is also

117

recommended that new born babies before their first birthday may be held by their mother or father for a short while, during their daily meditation sessions. Programmes have also been designed to enable very young children between three to ten, to derive benefits from meditation and concentration exercises.

Meditation is beneficial to all people of all age-groups. The darkness of ignorance, the delusion of the ego, the negative forces created by repressed feelings, the conflicts created by lack of understanding and the frustration of leading unfulfilled lives – all of these can be neutralised and negated through meditation. In short, meditation can help to widen, deepen and heighten on your experience of life.

Visions come naturally to the
Sadhaka on the spiritual path to
God-realization. But the *Sadhaka*
should not attach much importance
to them, but strive until he reaches
the ultimate goal.

Mother Krishnabai

Do not try to measure your progress
by your experiences. Your real
progress can only be measured by
the change in your consciousness
and the change that this brings about
in your behaviour, attitude, reactions
and responses.

J. P. V.

Experiences During Meditation

The question is often asked by beginners, "What can I expect during meditation?"

Meditation opens up the possibility for several spiritual experiences. These may take the form of visions, feelings or memories that are not normally revealed to us in our ordinary state. However, you must not go into meditation *expecting* anything to happen. An open mind is the best accompaniment to meditation.

When you embark on the practice of meditation, you are likely to experience things to which you are not normally accustomed. These are indications of subtle layers of your consciousness opening up to your awareness.

Here are some of the experiences felt by a few practitioners:

1. Vision of light – and various colours and hues.
2. *Darshan* of one's *ishtadevata* or *guru*.
3. Vision of beautiful, tranquil locations like lakes, forests and mountains.
4. Feelings associated with laughter, joy or tears.
5. Physical reactions like chill, trembling, etc.
6. Feeling of utter peace and contentment.
7. Hearing of voices. These must be treated with caution. Impurity in the mind may lead to negative voices, and therefore, inner purification is necessary.

8. The smell of special fragrances.
9. The sound of bells and soft humming.
10. Revelations are made to some practitioners.
11. Some people even report that they are able to communicate with their loved ones who are no more.

These visions, voices, lights, colours and feelings are all generated from the subconscious. Thoughts that are strong and powerful get converted to visions. Deep, inner emotions are converted into feelings of laughter or tears.

The experiences you receive in meditation mark different stages of your *sadhana*. It is best to keep them to yourself, or discuss them with your *Guru*.

But remember, you must not try to measure your progress by your experiences. You must not look for spectacular experiences either. Your real progress can only be measured by the change in your consciousness and the change that this brings about in your behaviour, attitude, reactions and responses.

Relax your body and mind and let your Spirit soar high.

Remez Sasson

The demand for tranquilizers increases day by day. What is needed is to relax – if possible, twice every day.

J. P. V.

Relax! Relax! Relax!

Meditation begins with relaxation. Most of the time we are tense without realising it. Even when we go to sleep, our body and mind are not relaxed; we carry the tensions of the day with us and so do not have restful sleep. We wake up the next morning with a feeling of languor or fatigue. We do not feel fresh and strong to meet the challenges of the new day. This goes on day after day, and the tension keeps on accumulating, until it manifests itself in one physical illness or another. So many diseases of the present day – heart attack, high blood pressure, nervous breakdown, migraine, asthma – are due to the building up of tension. It has been rightly said that "people do not die of disease: they die of internal combustion." The demand for tranquilizers increases day by day. What is needed is to relax – if possible, twice every day.

There are many methods of relaxation; each person must follow the one that best suits him or her. Here is a simple, easy, eleven-step method:

1. Lie on your back on the floor (or a carpet). Or sit on the floor in a comfortable posture. Or in a chair with your feet gently touching the floor. Take a few deep breaths, exhaling each slowly, completely emptying the lungs.

2. Imagine yourself in the loving, immediate and personal presence of the Lord (your Beloved). You are sitting at His Lotus Feet with your arms girdling His ankles, your head resting on His feet. Say to yourself, "Here is true rest. Here is true relaxation. In Thy presence, fears and frustrations, worries and anxieties, depressions and disappointments, tensions and tribulations vanish as mist before the rising sun. I am relaxed."
Relax...relax...relax.

3. To relax a muscle, you must first tighten it, then let it go. As you let it go, it may, perhaps, help you to utter the words, "Let go, let go, let God!"

4. Turn your attention to the muscles around the eyes. Relax-relax-relax. Open the eyes and imagine that the eyelids have become heavy. Let them drop on the eyes. Lift them and let them shut three times.

5. Move on to the muscles around the mouth. Tighten them and let go. Relax-relax-relax.

6. Relax your facial muscles. Clench your teeth, then relax, letting your face go limp. Relax-relax-relax.

7. Repeat the process throughout the body: neck, right shoulder, elbow, forearm, wrist, hand, fingers, left shoulder, elbow, forearm, wrist, hand, fingers, back, chest, abdomen, buttocks, calves, ankles, feet, toes. Push your toes down toward the carpet, stretch and relax. Pull your feet up toward the legs, stretch and relax. Relax-relax-relax.

8. Breathe in and stretch your whole body, relax and exhale. Repeat this three times. Relax-relax-relax. You are calm, relaxed, peaceful, serene. You are resting at the Lotus Feet of the Lord calm, relaxed, peaceful, serene.

9. You are now lighter than air, moving upwards, upwards, floating as a cloud – calm, relaxed, peaceful, serene.
10. You are in the presence of the Lord. Offer this simple prayer: "Thou art by me, a living and radiant Presence, and I am relaxed, calm, peaceful, serene." Repeat the prayer a few times. You are now completely relaxed.
11. When you wish to close this exercise in relaxation, rub the palm of your hands together, place them gently on the eyelids, and gently open the eyes.

The body needs material food every day. The soul needs spiritual food.

Remez Sasson

The life of God is in us already: only we have to be conscious of it.

J. P. V.

A Simple Exercise

Our lives need to be renewed, if possible, daily – through contact with God. The rain of God's mercy pours everyday; and those of us who receive it are washed clean, renewed and re-strengthened for the struggle of life. May I suggest to you a simple exercise? Every morning, as you sit in silence, close your eyes and imagine the Life of God coursing though every part of your body, filling it through and through. The Life of God is in us already: we have to be conscious of it. Say to yourself: *Every moment the Life of God* – call Him by what Name you will, Krishna, Buddha, Christ, Guru Nanak: they are all so many names of Him who is Nameless – *is filling every nerve and cell and fibre of my being!*

Then begin with the head. Feel the Life of God coursing through your head, and say, "The Life of God is renewing, revitalizing my entire brain, every nerve and nerve centre, and the entire cerebro-spinal-system. And my brain thinks the thoughts of God. It thinks in obedience to the Moral Law...

"The Life of God is renewing the entire sensory system. It is revitalizing the eyes; and now my eyes see more clearly, more purely. God's Light shines in and through them: and God's light is the light of purity.

"God's Life is revitalizing my ears. They hear more clearly and they hear words that are good and noble; and they hear the music of God that thrills the universe from end to end...

"God's Life is revitalizing my nose... God's Life is revitalizing my throat. How sweetly it sings the Name of God and the songs of the saints of God! And it utters words that are sweet and true and helpful to humanity!"

Now pause for a moment. Then take in a deep breath and turn your attention to the lungs and the heart. Imagine the Life of God renewing, revitalizing, the chest and the heart. "The heart is the seat of emotions, and because God's Life is in it, I shall be emotionally balanced, calm and serene in every situation and circumstance of life."

Turn your attention to your arms and hands. They are the hands of God. They are instruments of God's help and healing in this world of suffering and pain.... Think of the stomach and other organs... Then come to your legs, knees and feet. The feet are now firmly set on the path of righteousness and self-realization.

After covering your entire body, concentrate once again on the heart. The heart is the Sanctuary of the Temple, the Abode of the Lord. And now imagine the Lord seated in the heart – for that is where He is already – His Love, His Wisdom, His Strength, His Intelligence, His Joy, His Peace, all centred there and reaching out to every part of your body, and outside to your dear and near ones, and to your friends and "foes" alike.

It will take you longer to read this than to put this simple exercise into practice. Repeat this exercise, as often as you can, during the day. But do it at least twice every day - in the morning and at night. And you will soon, very soon, see the effects of it. Your health will improve. Your mind will be more relaxed and alert. Your heart will be more responsive to the pain of others. And you will grow in fuller, richer, deeper consciousness of the presence of God. He will be more real to you than the things of this earth. New love and longing for Him will wake up within your heart. And you will aspire to dedicate all you are, and all you have, at His Lotus Feet for the service of suffering creation. You will live and move and have your being in the Joy and Peace of God. You will be blessed among the children of men.

Health, a light body, freedom from cravings, a glowing skin, sonorous voice, fragrance of body: these signs indicate progress in the practice of meditation.

Upanishad, Shvetashvatara

The curative powers and healing energies within us can be harnessed through meditation practices and used effectively to fight mental and physical ailments.

J. P. V.

Health And Healing Through Meditation

Thousands of aspirants and seekers practise meditation as a spiritual exercise. Meditation also has multiple beneficial effects: it helps to clean and purify the mind; it rids us of the killing tendency of stress and tension; it makes us more sensitive, more aware of ourselves, our lives and the purpose of living. Its ultimate benefit is that we draw close to our Higher Self and realise our own Divinity.

There is yet another aspect to meditation, which is now well researched and documented by leading medical practitioners in east and west – the therapeutic, healing effects of meditation.

It is now realised that the curative powers and healing energies within us, can be harnessed through meditation practices and used effectively to fight mental and physical ailments.

- Distinguished psychiatrists like Dr. Brian Weiss have used meditation techniques to handle patients with relationship issues and fear psychoses.
- Researchers at Harvard University have found that meditation can comfort the elderly, cure them of depression and in some cases, even prolong their lives.

- Dr. Dean Ornish, the world-renowned cardiologist, has coordinated a study which has revealed that in conjunction with the right diet and exercise, meditation can act as an excellent stress-reduction technique that can actually *reverse* coronary artery disease. The point to be emphasised is that diet and exercise *alone* cannot achieve this: they may *prevent* heart disease but cannot *reverse* it. Meditation can eliminate stress and tension and this is a crucial factor in reversing the damage caused to the heart initially.

This is not all. Researchers have found that the relaxation and stress-reduction brought about by meditation can also help alleviate disorders like insomnia, hypertension and migraine. It can also help people who wish to reduce obesity, quit smoking and give up alcohol. Meditation has also been recognised to aid in the process of fighting infections and chronic diseases. It also strengthens our immune system, thus warding off illness. Let me quote Dr. Brian Weiss:

> I'm quite convinced that regular meditation is a priceless tool for the recovery and maintenance of health, for the chemistry and physics of the body are indeed influenced by mental and spiritual energies. This is a new context for rethinking health care, and for utilising practices that release these curative energies.

Most spiritual teachers will agree on this: that all healing comes from within. After all, even doctors tell us that medication through drugs only relieves the symptoms, and does not always negate the cause of the illness. For example, it is known that there is no effective drug to kill any virus; when we take a course of antibiotics, we only try to stop secondary infections from affecting our already weakened system.

We also know that several of these drugs have the most disturbing and harmful side-effects, which will lead to unforeseen, long-term problems.

Meditation provides an excellent supportive therapy which complements conventional medication and treatment. People who meditate feel fitter and healthier; *patients* who meditate, get well quicker.

People often complain of mental and physical exhaustion; young executives face the problem of 'burn out'; many 'successful' men and women complain that they wake up every morning with stress. They are unable to sleep peacefully at night, thus depriving the body of the rest and relaxation it needs. Physical strain and mental worries add to this condition of emotionally and physically 'drained' feeling.

Meditation gives our nervous system an extra period of deep rest during our waking hours. So, if one meditates twice a day, one can actually compensate for a bad night's lack of sleep – thus making the day more productive.

For those of us who rely on statistics, researchers have measured the comparative benefits of sleep and relaxation through meditation. It is said that it takes four or five hours of good sleep to produce a drop of 8% in the metabolic rate; whereas during a 30-minute meditation, we achieve a drop between 10% and 20%.

The slow down in metabolic rate is, of course, related to the relaxation of the body.

This does not mean that we can do away with sleep. Meditation, remember, is a *waking* exercise, it helps to rest our nervous system while we are awake – and in this process, it revitalises us, quickens our intelligence, makes us more alert and more creative.

"I *think*, therefore, I *am*," said the great philosopher, Descartes. Thought is supreme in the human being — but it must also be acknowledged that excessive thinking can cause problems. After all, thoughts, actually produce waves which register in the brain as electrical activity. When this becomes excessive, it causes severe disturbance to the brain. We begin to feel tense, stressed and disturbed. Meditation reduces thought-activity, thus reducing the power of the electrical waves on the brain. We begin to feel calm, peaceful and serene.

Body and mind are thus revitalised and rejuvenated by meditation. It also helps to:

- Improve our sleeping patterns
- Increase blood circulation to vital organs
- Stimulate healthy hormones
- Optimise brain function
- Decrease dependency on drugs
- Cure harmful addictions
- Reverse the ageing process, slowing down the decay of brain cells.

The more man meditates upon good thoughts, the better will be his world and the world at large.

Confucius

If we think good thoughts – thoughts of love and compassion, beauty and joy, faith and freedom, peace and wisdom – we create heaven around ourselves.

J. P. V.

Sutras

(Thoughts For Meditation)

1) He who does My work, is devoted to Me, is void of attachment, and hath no hatred to any being – he cometh unto Me!

Bhagavad Gita

2) Dost thou still seek the pleasures of sex or stomach? Thou wilt not know *Brahman*, the Eternal God!

The Upanishads

3) If a man possessed the whole world, he would not be wealthy thereby, because it perishes and passes away.

Rabia

4) Though your life lasts a hundred years, you die like the short-lived man. The years swiftly pass!

Mahavira

5) With coarse food to eat, water to drink, and a bent arm for a pillow, happiness may still be found.

Confucius

6) Be in this world like a traveller, or like a passer-on, and reckon yourself as of the dead.

Muhammad

7) Which religion gives the greatest joy to God? That
    which giveth love and compassion to all creatures.

Vallabha Acharya

8) Seek and ye shall find!
    Neglect and ye shall lose!

Mencius

9) Many a man by his babble shows that he is empty,
    indeed. But a few there be who show by their
    silence that they are Divine.

Tauler

10) Forgiveness is the strength of the weak and
    ornament of the strong.

Chanakya

11) A bad thought is the most dangerous of thieves.

Chinese Saying

12) The beginnings of all things are small.

Cicero

13) Money spent on ourselves may be a millstone
    about the neck; spent on others it may give us
    wings like eagles.

R. D. Hitchcock

14) Loving-kindness is greater than laws; and the
    charities of life are more than all ceremonies.

Talmud

15) Two are the qualities of him who is self-controlled:
    1) forgiveness; and 2) gentleness.

Rajarishi Yudhisthira

16) When you cannot find peace in yourself, it is
    useless to look for it elsewhere.

La Rochefoucauld

17) The highest wisdom is never to worry about the future but to resign ourselves entirely to His Will.

Mahatma Gandhi

18) God is in thy heart, yet thou searchest for Him in the wilderness.

Guru Granth Sahib

19) Heaven and earth are impartial. They regard all creatures as sacred.

Lao Tse

20) O Lord! So bless me that, in all the changing vicissitudes of life, I may never lose sight of Thee.

J.P. V.

21) If a Jew breaks a leg, he should say, "Praise be to God that I did not break both legs."
If he breaks both legs, he should say, "Praise be to God that I did not break my neck."

Yiddish Proverb

22) Moral life is the backbone of spiritual life. There cannot be any spiritual life without a moral life.

Swami Sivananda

23) Long for God alone. He may or may not meet you. But long only for Him.

Jamshed Nusserwanji

24) Our greatest glory is not in never falling, but in rising every time we fall.

Confucius

25) Prayer does not change God, but changes him who prays.

Soren Kierkegaard

26) Keep your mind pure in the battlefield of life.

Rig Veda

27) Pray as if everything depended on God, and work as if everything depended on man.

Cardinal Francis

28) Be humble and thy prayer will pierce through all the clouds and reach the Throne of God.

Sadhu Vaswani

29) Never think that God's delays are God's denials. Hold on, hold fast, hold out. Patience is genius.

Comte de Buffon

30) The secret of happiness is not in doing what one likes, but in liking what one has to do.

James Barrie

31) If thou wilt indeed live, learn first to die!

Tukaram

32) He who hath no check upon his tongue hath not truth in his heart.

Kabir

33) You will have to give an account of every careless word you utter.

Mathew 12:36

34) In prayer what is essential is not words but the deep silence of communion.

J.P.V.

35) Wouldst thou win purity? Then cleanse thyself with these three: good thoughts, good words, good deeds.

Zoroaster

36) Turn thine eyes into thyself and beware thou judge not the deeds of others!

Thomas a Kempis

37) The wise man does not teach by words but by deeds.

Lao Tse

38) Meditation on God is my food: His Praise is my drink: and to bear witness to His Glory is my garment.

Junnuna Misri

39) Happy is the Muslim, for if good befalls him, he thanks God; and if evil befalls him, he praises God and bears his misfortune patiently.

Muhammad

40) Let's reform the world, shouts the social worker. Fine, agrees the saint, you reform yourself, I reform myself, and immediately the world is better.

Anonymous

41) He who hears the inner voice within him has no need to listen to outer words.

Jallaludin

42) Every man feels instinctively that all the beautiful sentiments in the world weigh less than a single lovely action.

James Russell Lowell

43) Man has been endowed with two ears and one tongue, that he may listen more than speak.

Abraham Hasdai

44) Time goes, you say? Ah no! Alas, time stays, we go.

Austin Dobson

45) God's plan is perfect, and whatever happens is for the best.

J.P. V.

46) The Self cannot be gained by knowledge.

Katha Upanishad

47) If thou wilt know thyself, lose thyself in love! And thou wilt find thyself.

Sadhu Vaswani

48) He that sinneth, sinneth unto himself.
He that is unjust, hurts himself, in that he makes himself worse than he was before.

Marcus Aurelius

49) It is not the knowing that is difficult, but the doing.

Chinese Proverb

50) All beings feel pleased by sweet speech: one should therefore talk sweet.
What does it cost to do so?

Chanakya

51) Naughty or good, I am Thy child. Sinner or saint, I am Thy child.

Paramahansa Yogananda

52) I am always with myself; and it is I who am my tormentor.

Leo Tolstoy

53) Three are the gateways of hell leading to the ruin of the soul: lust, wrath and greed. Therefore, let man renounce these three.

Bhagavad Gita

54) We cannot be certain of living the next minute. But we are not content with even a million plans.

Kural

55) Everything is God. Good fortune is God; misfortune is God. Greet Him in everything and rest peacefully in bliss.

Swami Sivananda

56) All that a man bears for God's sake, God makes light and sweet for him.

Meister Eckhart

57) Allah is in the East and Allah is in the West; wherever you turn there is Allah's Face!

The Qur'an

58) The sages look alike on all – a learned Brahmin, a cow, an elephant, a dog, or an outcast!

Bhagavad Gita

59) In every form behold the One Face of Beauty. To see aught else is a sin!

Sachal

60) However men approach Me, even so do I greet them as Mine own: for all the paths men take from any side are Mine, verily Mine!

Bhagavad Gita

61) If the Mussalman understood what the idol really was, he would know that there was true religion in idolatry.

Mahmud of Sabister

62) See ye what I behold? Verily, the Lord hath become the One-in-all, the All-in-one!

Sri Ramakrishna Parmahansa

63) Blessed is the way of the Helpers. They are the companions of Christ!

H. Van Dyke

64) We gain only as we give.

Simms

65) Men resemble the gods in nothing so much as in doing good to their fellow-creatures.

Cicero

66) The highest freedom consists in complete devotion to God. With God begin, with God complete the day.

Tolmachev

67) The greatest tragedy of man is – he thinks he has plenty of time.

J.P. V.

68) Half, if not two-thirds, of our ailings and diseases are the fruits of our imagination and fears.

H.P. Blavatsky

69) There are three things with which wisdom cannot exist: covetousness, licentiousness, and pride.

Welsh Triad

70) Lord Zoroaster showed two ways to conserve purity: control of temper and hard labour.

Jamshed Nusserwanji

71) All sins are committed in secrecy. The moment we realize that God witnesses even our thoughts we shall be free.

Mahatma Gandhi

72) That person will not enter paradise who hath one atom of pride in his heart.

Muhammad

73) Happiness does not consist in things but in thoughts.

Booth

74) Prayer is conscious union with Cosmic Intelligence. Prayer is not supplication; it is Oneness.

Julian Seton Sears

75) Beware! Beware! Your actions will recoil on your own head!

Tseng Tze

76) There is one Instructor; there is no second different from Him. I speak concerning Him who abides in the heart.

Anu Gita

77) Rabbi Eleazer said, "Repent one day before your death."
Said his pupils, "Does man know when he would die?" He answered, "Then he surely must repent today, lest he die tomorrow."

Anonymous

78) The way to rise in the scale of evolution is to raise others. The secret of achievement is self-effacement.

Sadhu Vaswani

79) In all situations of life, keep calm. The inner balance is essential to spiritual progress.

J.P.V.

80) He is not a perfect Muslim who eats his fill and lets his neighbour go hungry.

Muhammad

81) In all the world there is no such thing as a stranger.

Kurosumi Kyo

82) Behold the man who killeth not and who abstaineth from flesh-meat. All the world joineth hands and riseth to do him reverence.

Kural

83) The Sufi has no individual will. His will is merged in the Will of God; his will becomes the very Will of God!

Jami

84) True love means to give all that thou hast to Him whom thou lovest, so that nothing remains to thee of thine own.

Abu Abdallah Al Qurashi

85) Harmonious living is more important than doing deeds of service.

J.P.V.

86) When the heart weeps for what it has lost, the spirit laughs for what it has found.

Abu Sulayman

87) In this broad, boundless sea of life, Thou art my Boat. How can I cross without Thee Beloved?

Mira

88) There is no problem that cannot be solved. In God is the solution to all problems.

J.P.V.

89) It is better to have a heart without words, than words without a heart.

Mahatma Gandhi

90) When obstacles and trials seem like prison walls to me, I do the little I can do, and leave the rest to Thee.

F.W. Faber

91) Which is the quickest – and easiest – way to God? The way of Love!

J.P.V.

92) The Self is dearer than a son, dearer than wealth, dearer than all else, and is the innermost.

Brihadaranyaka Upanishad

93) Be humble and gentle in your conversation, and of few words; and meddle not into other folk's matters.

William Penn

94) I am the Father of the whole universe, the Mother, the Creator, the Lord, the Friend.

Bhagavad Gita

95) Proceed on the axiom that all are godly, and everyone will behave as God if you behave as God towards them.

Swami Rama Tirtha

96) Be doers of the Word, and not merely hearers.

James 1:22

97) When God loves a servant, He proves him by suffering.

Hudayfa B. Husayl Al-Yaman

98) My rule of life: Love God and serve the Brotherhood!

St. Parks Cadman

99) Thou art not safe until thou hast surrendered thyself wholly to the Lord!

Sadhu Vaswani

100) You may have a number of appointments to keep every day. Never forget to keep your daily appointment with God!

J.P.V.

By the practice of meditation you will find that you are carrying within your heart a portable paradise.

Yogananda

Many there are who wish to meditate but do not know how.

J. P. V.

Guided Meditations

Guided mediation sessions form an integral part of the programmes at Sadhu Vaswani Mission's Sadhana Camps (spiritual camps), held in both Eastern and Western lands. Retreatants meet together in a hall and are guided, step by step, with the help of audiotapes.

The following few examples, adapted for this book, have been used with good results; perhaps they will help you.

Meditation On Awareness

This meditation calms the restless and agitated mind and helps in increasing the power to concentrate on work, studies and spiritual development. But it is not as simple as it may seem on the surface.

Let us relax. One of the main obstacles on the path of meditation is physical tension. There are many who believe that meditation is only a means: that the end is relaxation. Actually, it is the other way round. Relaxation is the means: meditation is the goal. Try to relax every muscle, every nerve, every limb, of the body – make the body tension-free. Relax the mind as well: let it be free of fear, anxiety, frustration, worry, depression, disappointment. Even as a towel is wrung to drain it of every drop of water, so let the mind, pictured in the form of a towel, be drained of all tension, drop by drop.

We are now ready to embark on a spiritual journey that, with God's grace, will take us into the depths within and give us that which surpasses understanding.

As I have mentioned before, in the beginning of such exercises you will find your attention often wanders. The Cistercian monk, Thomas Keating, describes this wandering as "woolgathering" and says it is caused by the imagination's "propensity for perpetual motion". For some time, you may not even be conscious of the wandering. But as soon as you do become aware, gently bring back your attention to your breath, as it enters and leaves the nostrils.

You will be amazed at how many and how trivial these wanderings can be. The mind keeps jumping from one place to another, from one object to another. Hopes, fears and memories pass through the mind in a seemingly endless procession. We do not have to fight the mind. In fact, we cannot fight the mind: it can be a very powerful adversary. We have to humour it. We have to bring the mind back, gently and lovingly, to our breathing.

As we breathe, let us *actually* feel the air coming in and flowing out of our nostrils. Keep all attention on the tip of the nostrils.

The attention has wandered from the tip of the nostrils. Gently, very gently, bring it back to the breathing. Be alert!

Be relaxed and let the face wear a soft smile.

Do not interfere with the breathing: merely watch it. Watch the breath as it comes in and flows out at the tip of the nostrils.

This is an exercise in awareness. We do not have to control the breath; we have only to watch it. Be relaxed and let the face wear a soft smile. And be alert!

Remain silent for about three minutes.

You have now meditated for seventeen minutes. The period of silence is over. Rub the palms of your hands together, softly place them on your eyelids, and gently open your eyes. *Om, shanti, shanti, shanti!*

Meditation On Death

Let us, for a brief while, forget the world – its worries and woes, problems and perplexities – and feel that we are in the loving, the immediate, the personal presence of God. God is not far from us. He is wherever we are. He is here, He is now. All we have to do is close our eyes, shut out the world, open our heart, and call Him. And He is here in front of us!

Let us begin this meditation with a short prayer:

Lord, I need You! I love You!
I want to love You more than anything in the world!
I want to love You so that I may be lost in You completely!
Grant me pure love and devotion for Your Lotus Feet,
And so bless me that this world-bewitching *maya* may not lead me astray.

And make me, Blessed Master, an instrument of Your help and healing in this world of suffering and pain!

Now let us relax. Relax every muscle, every limb, every nerve in the body. Make it tension-free. If you like, you may mentally picture the body in the form of a huge sack of potatoes. The sack is cut at the middle, allowing the potatoes to roll out. How relaxed is the empty sack! Let the body feel relaxed likewise.

Now let the mind be free of worries of the past and fears or expectations of the future. Let us live in the present – the here and the now!

Now let us sit in a comfortable posture, so that we will not need to change it, for a period of about twenty-five to thirty minutes. Let us sit comfortably, preferably in a cross-legged position, and keep our spine erect. If you wish, you can sit in a chair, keeping your spine erect and your feet gently touching the floor.

Now take in three deep breaths. As you breathe deeply, be relaxed. Begin. Breathe in slowly, deeply...(pause).

Now exhale slowly, completely... (pause).

Now blend your breathing with the repetition of the sacred syllable "*Om*". First fill your lungs quickly, then, as you slowly let out the breath, utter the sacred word "*Om*". One-third of the utterance should be with parted lips, and the remaining two-thirds with lips closed. This will create a vibration within you. Do this three times. Take in the breath quickly, then slowly let out the breath and utter "*Om*"

Om ...

Om ...

Om ...

Now let us meditate a little on the transitoriness of life. No one can stay on earth forever, but so many, alas, live in mortal fear of death. So many are afraid of death. We forget that birth and death are but two sides of the same coin. Wherever there is birth, there is bound to be death. Whoever is born must die. Leaving the body is called death, even as entering the body is called birth. Death applies only to the physical body. When the body drops down, when the body dies, we do not die. We are immortal, eternal, deathless. It is the body that dies.

151

As Lord Sri Krishna says in the *Bhagavad Gita*, the body is only a garment that we have worn. The garment drops down, the garment becomes useless, but the wearer of the garment continues to live. From now on, never say that you will die. It is the physical body that dies. The *jiv-atman* – the soul that wears the physical body – continues to live in the life that is undying. Once you understand this, you will never be afraid of death. The root cause of our fear is our identification with the physical body. We have identified ourselves with our physical bodies. The physical body is only a house in which we dwell for a brief period. The house crumbles; the tenant of the house continues to live on. He lives in some other house.

Now let us consider a little of the experience through which a person passes when the physical body dies. In the moment of death, God will appear to us in the Form in which we have thought of Him. In the moment of death, that Form of Light will appear to us and, with tender, love-filled eyes, will look at us and will put to us the question, "My child! What have you done with your life?" In that moment, we will realise that life was given to us as a gift from God for a special purpose. Alas, lured by temptations, entangled by desire, pulled by passion, we completely forgot this purpose. We squandered our life, we chased shadow-shapes that came and went. We ran after pleasures and possessions and power and, in the process, turned away, again and again, from the Light. We bartered the precious thing called life for transitory joys and ephemeral possessions. We earned nothing. And now we stand in the presence of God, empty-handed. What answer may we give to His question, "My child! What have you done with your life?"

There is comfort in the thought that it is not yet too late. So long as there is breath in this body, so long do we have the opportunity to fulfill the purpose for which we have been sent to the earth-plane. Therefore, let us spend some time in silence and ask ourselves the question, "Who am I? What is the purpose of my visit to the earth-plane? Where am I moving? Am I drifting away or am I drawing nearer to the goal?" When we set out on a long journey, we take along money and provisions. When we have to appear for an examination, we first study hard to be able to show brilliant results. The journey of death, the inevitable journey that none of us can avoid, is the greatest journey we shall ever undertake. Shall we set out on the journey empty-handed?

Sant Gnaneshwar says, "As long as you can speak, let your words be kind! Before the hands become paralysed, let us keep on giving as much as we can! As long as the mind can work, let us think pure, noble, holy thoughts! And, above all, let us arrange our house while the lamp is yet burning!" Soon the night comes, when no one can work. Let every day of our life be a day of preparation. *Prepare! Prepare!* This is the one word that our dear ones on the Other Side wish to pass on to us. *Prepare! Prepare!* For they find us chasing things that, to them, are no better than shadows. They find us running after money, trying to gather millions, not a single penny of which we will be allowed to carry with us into the Great Beyond. They find us running after pleasures and sense-enjoyments – after name, fame, greatness and earthly glory. These are all shadows. So they ask us to open our eyes, to wake up from the slumber of the senses and the mind, and prepare for the inevitable journey, the journey that awaits us.

1. Let us establish a link of love and devotion with someone who, to us, is a symbol of Truth or God. Let us establish a link of love and devotion with God Himself. Every day, let us strengthen this link of love and devotion. Every day, let us pray to Him, let us kiss His Holy Feet, let us offer all our work to Him, let us, in moments of silence, converse with Him, in love and with intimacy. Let this link grow, from more to more, until we feel that, wherever we are, we are not far from Him. We are overshadowed by His radiant presence. And in His presence there can be no death. For when this body drops down, He will be by us, and He will lift us in His loving, everlasting arms, and He will lead us on – ever onward, forward, Godward.

2. As we establish this link of love and devotion with God, we shall realize that in everything that happens, there is a meaning of God's mercy. Many things happen in life: we are unable to understand the "why" of them. Suddenly our dear ones are snatched away from us, suddenly a misfortune overtakes us. Instead of wasting our time and energy in enquiring why such a bitter experience entered our life, let us move forward to greet every incident and accident, every illness and adversity, every misfortune and calamity, with the words, "I accept! I accept!"

3. Let us be a blessing to others. In the measure in which we become unselfish, in that measure our heart expands. Those who lead selfish lives on earth, those who harm others to get little advantages for themselves, find themselves imprisoned in tiny, dark cells when they move to the Other Side. Therefore, let us live unselfishly! Let us be a blessing to others!

If God has blessed us with wealth and abundance, with position and power, it is so that we may be a blessing to others. Receiving without giving makes a person full and proud and selfish. Give out the best in yourself, in God's Name, for the good of others. The day on which I have not helped someone – a brother here or a sister there – to lift the load on the rough road of life is a lost day, indeed.

Let us come back to the picture on which each one of us will meditate today. In the moment of death, I stand in the radiant presence of God, the Being of Light, who looks at me with tender, understanding, love-filled eyes, and puts to me the question, "My child! What have you done with your life?" *"My child! What have you done with your life?"*

Remain silent for ten minutes.

By God's grace, the period of silence is now over. Now let us rub the palms of our hands together, place them softly on the eyelids, and gently, open the eyes.

Om shanti, shanti, shanti!

Meditation On Self-Surrender

Let us for a brief while forget the world, forget its worries and vexations, its tensions and tribulations and feel that we are in the presence of God. God is always with us. We are not always with God. We forget Him again and again. Therefore, we must practise the presence of God. Everytime we find our thoughts straying away from God, let us bring the mind gently, lovingly back into the Divine Presence. Before we begin the meditation, let us offer a small, simple prayer: O Lord, may our senses be free from the drag of sense

155

objects. May our minds sit still in the Divine Presence as a bee sucking honey out of a flower. May our intellect, the *buddhi*, be illumined with the Light of the *Atman*. May our entire being be filled with Light. Light, Light. Light in front, Light behind, Light to the right, Light to the left, Light above, Light below, Light within, Light all around. Light, Light, Light.

Now let us sit in a comfortable posture so that we will not need to change it, say for a period of 20 to 30 minutes. Let us sit straight with the neck, the head and the back in a straight line. And now let us take in three deep breaths. As you breathe deeply, be relaxed.

Now begin.

Now let us utter the sacred name, the sacred syllable *Om* three times. Take in a deep breath and as you take it out utter the sacred syllable, *Om*.

O.................M.

O.................M.

O.................M.

Now visualize Lord Krishna standing on the banks of the river Jamuna. On His lips is the flute. Krishna is the Divine Self in the heart of everyone. God is the Formless One. But for the sake of His devotees, He has worn many Forms and visited the earthplane again and again and still again. One of these many Forms is Krishna. Krishna is not separate from other Forms of God. He is not separate from Rama. He is not separate from Buddha. He is not separate from Jesus and other Forms of the Eternal One. No separation. Our reverence and love, our *bhakti* and *shraddha* must move out to every form of God. They all are one! They all are one! They all are one!

Come back to Sri Krishna playing on the Flute by the banks of the Jamuna river. Krishna's blue complexion symbolizes infinity. His flute, made out of a hallow bamboo reed, stands for the devotees who would be hollow – empty of the ego. If we are emptied of the ego, the Lord takes us up and through us, sings His song for the healing of the human race. Can there be a greater blessing? Can there be a higher privilege than this? There are anklets on Krishna's Feet. As He walks, anklets jingle and produce a soothing sound. Every step that we take *must* bring comfort to a weary heart. Around Krishna's neck is a rosary – *Tulsi mala* reminding us that we are not completely dressed until we keep on repeating the Name Divine.

Hare Shyam! Hare Shyam! Shyam, Shyam, Hare, Hare!
Hare Krishna! Hare Krishna! Krishna, Krishna, Hare, Hare!

Hare Shyam! Hare Shyam! Shyam, Shyam, Hare, Hare!
Hare Krishna! Hare Krishna! Krishna, Krishna, Hare, Hare!

Hare Shyam! Hare Shyam! Shyam, Shyam, Hare, Hare!
Hare Krishna! Hare Krishna! Krishna, Krishna, Hare, Hare!

By the side of the Lord is a cow. The cow symbolizes the *Bhagavad Gita* and other world scriptures. Each cow gives its own type of milk. But the milk of every cow has the same colour. The inspiration of all scriptures is the same. The wisdom of all scriptures is one. In the *Bhagavad Gita* the Lord gives us the essence of all the scriptures.

Let us take up one *sloka* of the *Bhagavad Gita*. Say, for instance, that *sloka* in the 18th *Adhyaya* in which the Lord says, "*Sarvadharman parityajya mamekam sharnam vraja*" – "Renouncing all rites and writ duties, come to Me for single refuge. I shall liberate you, O Arjuna! I shall liberate you from all bondage to sin and suffering, of this have no doubt."

Let us meditate on this *sloka*, let us enter into the depths of the meanings contained in the meaning of this *sloka*. Let us try to understand what it is to seek refuge at the Lotus Feet of the Lord. Let us say to Him, out of the very depths of our heart, "Lord I come to Thee as I am. Full of faults and failings, failures and frailities, full of weaknessess and imperfections I come to Thee. I come to Thee as I am. *Hari mein jesso, tesso, Tero. Hari mein jesso, tesso, Tero.* Accept me and make of me what Thou wilt. I shall not complain but I shall accept Thy Will and rejoice in all the changing vicissitudes of life. In health and sickness, in prosperity and adversity, in praise and censure, in cold and heat, out of the very depths of my heart will come this one prayer again and again, "In sun and rain, in loss and gain, in pleasure and pain, Thy Will be done! Thy Will be done! Thy Will be done!

Ten Minutes Silence

The period of silence is over. And now let us rub the palms of our hands together and gently, very gently, softly, very softly touch them on the eyes and open them. *Om shanti, shanti, shanti!*

Meditation of Six Steps

This meditation lasts 15 to 20 minutes. It is a meditation of six steps. Each step will take roughly two minutes and a half to about three minutes. I will first explain to you all the steps and then you can start. The first is the step of *rhythmic* breathing. Breathe in slowly, easily, evenly and deeply. And then, breathe out slowly, easily, evenly and deeply. Within 3 minutes, you should be able to breathe in and out about 10 times. And when the three minutes are over, I shall ask you to move on to the second step. As your breathing becomes rhythmic, your tensions will relax. It may be better if you blend the repetition of *Om* with your breathing. As you inhale – take in the breath, utter the sacred syllable *Om* silently. Then exhale – take out the breath and as you do so, utter the sacred syllable, *Om* orally, that is with sound.

The second is the step of *detached observation*. In this step, as an observer, you have to watch the movements of the mind. Detach yourself from the mind. This is very, very important. You are not the mind, you are only watching the mind. What is the mind doing? What thoughts is it entertaining? You are not the mind. You are not thinking those thoughts. Just watch the mind. Observe the mind without any judgement, without any criticism. You are only a silent observer. Observe without judgement, without criticism. You will find that as you detach yourself from the mind and just keep on watching it – its movements – gradually the mind will cease its activities.

Then we come to the third step – the third step is the step of *serenity*, the step of peace. In this third step you may imagine yourself as a rock in the midst of an ocean. Waves arise. Waves are the distracting thoughts. Waves arise. They dash against the rock. The rock is unaffected, is calm, tranquil, peaceful, serene.

Then we come to the fourth step. It is the step where you realize your *oneness* with all that is – all men, all creatures, all things, all conditions. You are not apart from others. The others and you are but parts of the One Great Whole. You are in every man, in every woman, in every child. You are in every unit of life, in every bird and animal, in every fowl and fish, in every insect, in every shrub, in every plant. You belong to all

159

countries and communities, all races and religions. You are at one with the universe. This type of meditation will fill your heart with loving kindness, and a spirit of compassion so that a stage may come when you will not wish to snuff out the life even of the smallest insect.

The fifth step is meditation on your *immortality*. In the fourth step you have realized that you are not merely in your physical body, you are in all that is. In the experience that we call death, it is the body that drops down, but you will continue to be. You will continue to live in every grain of sand, in every drop of water, in every ray of sunshine. Death cannot touch you. You are immortal. If you are at one with all humanity, then even if there is but one human being alive, you are alive. If you are at one with all living creatures, then even if there is but one creature breathing the breath of life, you are alive. Yes, you are immortal, immutable, eternal, deathless.

And now we come to the final, the last, the sixth step. In this step you *breathe out peace and happiness, goodwill and bliss to all*. May all be happy and full of peace and bliss. Think of all who dwell in northern lands and pray in the heart within, "May all who dwell in northern lands be happy and full of peace and bliss." Then think of all who dwell in southern lands and offer the prayer, "May all who dwell in southern lands be happy and full of peace and bliss." Likewise, "May all who dwell in eastern lands, and all who dwell in western lands, may they all be happy and full of peace and bliss." Breathe out peace and goodwill to all. May all be happy and full of peace and bliss. All living things, whether they be near or far, tall or tiny, rich or poor, educated or illiterate, whether they be born or are still in the womb unborn, may all, all, all be happy and full of peace and bliss. May those that love you, and those that, for some reason or the other, are unable to love you, may those that speak well of you, and those that, for some reason or the other, are unable to speak well of you – may all, all, all without exception – be happy and full of peace and bliss. You are in them all. It is only when they become happy that you are happy. May all be free from disease, ignorance, sorrow. As you get up from this meditation, you will find that you yourself are happy and full of peace and bliss.

And now, if you are ready, we shall begin the meditation. Sit in a relaxed posture. As far as possible, the back, the neck and the head should be in a straight line. In the beginning you may find it difficult to bring them all in a straight line, but do it as far as possible. Above all, be relaxed. Relax your body, relax your muscles, relax your limbs. And now let us embark on this interior journey – a journey that takes us within – a journey that, in due course, may change our life and fill us with tranquillity, with peace and bliss and make us instruments of God's help and healing in this world of suffering and pain.

The first step is the step of rhythmic breathing – therefore breathe in slowly, easily, evenly, deeply, as deeply as possible. And to make your breathing deep, one thing that will help you is, when you exhale, try to breathe out as much as possible. Now take the first step. Empty the lungs as far as possible. Now inhale – take in the breath and utter the sacred syllable, *Om* – silently. Then exhale – take out the breath and as you do so, utter the sacred syllable *Om* orally – with sound. Begin. Inhale.

Exhale O…..M.O…..M.O…..M.O…..M.O…..M.O…..
M.O….. M.O….. M.O…..M…

Some of you feel so relaxed and at peace that you would love to be in this state for a longer period. When you do your individual meditation, you can increase this period. Now we come to the second step. It is the step of detached observation. Detach yourself from the mind. Watch the movements of the mind. Don't get involved with the mind. You are not the mind, you are only a silent observer. Watch the mind without any judgement. No judgement. This is very, very important. Only observe the mind. Watch the movements of the mind, watch them, don't get involved with the mind. You are not the mind, you are only a silent observer. Watch the movements of the mind even as you would watch the movements of a little child who is being naughty. Don't pay attention to your breathing. Only watch the movements of the mind. Just watch the mind sitting easily in a relaxed posture, watch what the mind is doing.

Silence

Don't pay attention to the breathing. Only watch the movements of the mind. Watch as a silent observer. Watch without judgement.

Silence

Be relaxed. See that the muscles around the eyes and those around the mouth are relaxed. Relax! Relax! Relax! Relax!

Silence

The next three minutes and half are over. We have had in all, six minutes of meditation. We move on to the third step. It is the step of serenity and peace. I imagine that I am like a rock in the midst of an ocean.

Waves arise, distracting thoughts come to me, they dash against the rock. But the rock is unaffected, unmoved, calm, tranquil, peaceful, serene. So many waves come. Perhaps, I have done something during the day which I should not have done, let that not disturb me. I am a rock in the midst of an ocean, unaffected, unmoved, calm, tranquil, peaceful, serene. Perhaps, I have not done something which I should have done, let that not disturb me either. I am a rock in the midst of an ocean, unaffected, unmoved, calm, tranquil, peaceful, serene. Calm, tranquil, peaceful, serene.

Silence

Some past memory comes to me. Let that not affect me. I am a rock in the midst of an ocean. Calm, tranquil, peaceful, serene. Calm, tranquil, peaceful, serene.

Silence

Don't pay attention to your breathing. Don't watch the movements of the mind. You have only to imagine that you are a rock in the midst of an ocean unaffected by anything that may have happened. Unaffected by anything that may happen. You are like a rock in the midst of an ocean. Calm, tranquil, peaceful, serene. Calm, tranquil, peaceful, serene.

Silence

We now come to the fourth step. It is the step of realizing my oneness with all that is. All human beings, all creatures, all birds and animals, fish and fowl, insects, even mosquitoes, all trees, and shrubs and plants. I am one with them all. I am in the lowliest of the low, in the poorest of the poor. I am in the meanest of the mean, in the most wretched, the most miserable. I am in Him. He is not apart from me. Oneness, Oneness with all. Out of this cometh true love. If I am One with all, I am in the lizard of which I am afraid. I am in the cockroach which I want to kill. I am in all. I am in all. I am in all. How can I kill anyone? How can I criticise anyone? How can I judge anyone? How can I think ill of anyone? I am in all that is. What a wonderful feeling is this! No one is apart from me. Everyone, everything is a part of me, for I am the Universal Self – *tat twam asi.* That art thou! Thou art not the physical body that thou hast worn during this period of earth-incarnation. Thou art That. Thou art That. The Universal Self. Relax! Relax! Relax! Let your back bone be straight.

Silence

And now we come to the fifth step. If I am in all, if I have realised my oneness with all, I can never, never die. It is only when I feel I am this physical body that I live in fear of death. Now I can challenge death. Death! You cannot touch me, you can take away this physical body but I am in all. So long as there is one human being alive on earth, I am alive. So long as there is a leaf fluttering in the wind, I am alive. I can never, never die. I have never died. I am eternal, I am immortal, I am immutable, I am deathless. I am in every ray of sunshine, in every drop of rain, in every grain of sand. I am One with all that is.

Silence

By now your breathing has become deep. Be relaxed. See that your spine is straight. See that there is no tension in the muscles round your eyes and round your mouth. See that there is no tension in the muscles of your legs. Relax! Relax! Relax!

Silence

You are not the physical body. You are not the body-mind complex. You are The Universal Self. The One Self that is in all, in all that is.

Silence

And now we come to the final step, the sixth step, the step in which we breathe out love and goodwill and peace to all. "I love you all! I love you all!" Let that aspiration come out of the very depths of my heart. In the measure in which I give love to the others, love will flow back to me and I will always have plenty of love to give to everyone who meets me. Love all in the northern countries, in the southern countries, in the western countries, in the eastern countries. I love everyone. I love you! I love you! And I pray that you all may be happy, full of peace and bliss. I love those that love me and also who, for some reason or the other, are unable to love me. I love those that speak well of me and also those who, for some reason or the other, are unable to speak well of me. Actually call out someone by name, someone who you think does not love you, does not speak well of you, and say, "Mr. X, Y, Z, Mrs. X, Y, Z, Miss. X, Y, Z, I love you! I love you! I love you! I love you all." May you all be happy and full of peace and bliss!

Silence

And now must come the final benediction. May all, all, all without exception be free from disease, free from ignorance, free from sorrow.

As you get up from this mediation, many of you will feel that you yourself are happy, full of peace and bliss.

Now let us rub the palms of our hands together. Place them gently on the eye-lids and gently, very, very gently open the eyes. That is the end of this meditation of six steps.

You yourself must make an effort.
The Great Ones are only teachers.

Buddha

Aspire, aspire! This is the law of
spiritual life: whatever you aspire for,
will come to you.

J. P. V.

Meditation Exercises For You

1) Meditation On Contentment, Abundance And Fulfillment

Many of us simply can't get enough of certain things – love, affection, attention, money, wealth, possessions, opportunities, openings and possibilities.

This often leads to a feeling of deprivation, lack, want.

And this is so needless, so futile!

We live in a world of abundance that God has created, and He has given us enough and more to meet all our needs and to share with those who need them more than we do!

Step 1: Follow the first basic procedures until you are seated comfortably and focused inward.

Step 2: For the next 10-15 minutes, imagine that you are receiving positive energy from the Universe with every breath you inhale.

Allow your consciousness to open to its full receptivity, in order to gather this shower of positive forces that is being poured upon you in abundance.

Experience the flow of light, love, wealth and energy.

Let it flow over you, wash you, surround you and fill your spirit.

Step 3: For the final few minutes, just allow yourself to revel in this shower of abundance. Absorb the positive energies. Allow it to permeate to the very core of your being. Feel yourself fulfilled to overflowing. Become aware, as you prepare to move, that this abundance is yours to keep forever; and that it is always available to you for the asking.

2)   Meditation On Forgiveness And Letting Go

They tell me that one of my books which has sold most worldwide is *Burn Anger Before Anger Burns You* – Published by Gita Publishing House, 10, Sadhu Vaswani Path, Pune – 411001. India.

This points to the reality that anger and resentment darken our lives to such an extent that we do not know how to free ourselves from its terrible shadows.

The escape lies through the healing path of forgiveness.

Forgiveness can liberate you, set you free from the clutches of wrath, resentment and bitterness.

Step 1: Follow the first basic procedures until you are seated comfortably and focussed inward.

Step 2: Meditate on the following image:

Picture a bright merry fire that you have lit in a courtyard.

Contemplate the fire for a few minutes. Fire burns and destroys; it also purifies.

What would you like to throw into the fire, so that it is destroyed forever? Think of the anger, resentment and bitterness that are pent up in you. Think of all the unhappiness and distress they have caused you. Isn't it time these were destroyed in the bright, dancing flames?

Picture yourself throwing your negative emotions in the fire, one by one. Anger, envy, resentment, jealousy…

Notice the fire flaring up as these negative emotions are destroyed. Watch the flames consume all that is unpleasant and negative. Watch it all turn to ashes…

The fire has not only destroyed your anger and resentment. It has purified your heart by cleansing the clutter of unforgiving attitudes.

Stir the ashes. Make sure everything is burnt up. When the embers have died and the ashes are cold, clean them away. Sweep your courtyard clean.

Step 3: End your meditation with deep breathing. Exhale love and peace to the whole world. Inhale love and joy from the process of interior purification. Allow a feeling of peace, tolerance, understanding and sympathy to descend on you. Arise with the contented feeling that you hold no resentment within you: that you have forgiven everything and everyone.

3) Meditation On Patience

Have you heard of the beautiful prayer, "God, give me the power to change the things I can, accept the things that I cannot change, and the wisdom to know the difference?"

Alas, we spend much of our time and energy trying to control things which we cannot control. The futile effort leaves us frustrated, impatient and embittered.

We need to develop the virtues of patience and acceptance – not as passive, helpless victims, but as wise and understanding human beings.

Tolerance, understanding, acceptance: the world has great need of these today. Above all, we need to be patient with ourselves!

Step 1: Follow the basic procedures until you are seated comfortably and focussed inward.

Step 2: Picture a rose bud that is about to bloom. Watch the petals unfold, open up in slow motion. Watch the plant stay still as the rose opens up. Watch the earth hold the plant's roots firmly in place as the rose blooms. Watch the sky bent silently over the scene.

Everything has its time and place. All the world revolves at God's pace, with God's grace, according to His Will.

Accept! Accept! Accept! Do not let the waves of frustration and impatience meddle with the beautiful blooming of the rose. Let nature take its course. Let life unfold as God wills.

Step 3: As you come out of meditation, breathe out understanding, love and harmony to all the world. As you inhale, breathe in the joyous spirit of patience and acceptance.

4)   Meditation On Reconciliation And Restoring Relationships

Human relationships are at once subtle, delicate and complex. When the going is good, everything is smooth and hassle-free; loving warmth and affection, friendship and understanding flourish. But when things begin to go wrong, the ride becomes rough. The human tendency is to shift the blame, accuse the other person and assume the role of the injured party, and, in general, feel that one is the victim and the other is miscreant. In short, negative tendencies take over the human psyche, and the relationship suffers. This happens to everyone, at one time or another in life – between parents and children, between husband and wife, siblings, friends, partners and colleagues.

Relationships need to be healed and treated, as much as the people involved in them. We need to change our attitude; we need to think positively; we need to cultivate a deeper spiritual understanding in order to enrich our relationships, to heal them and make them whole again. This becomes even more important when our relationships are broken and bruised by misunderstandings.

John Sanford, a reputed analyst, tells us, "Healing is a cooperative venture between the conscious personality and the unconsciousness."

We need to rid ourselves of persecution complex; we need to come out of the victim-trap and develop emotional maturity. We will then find our perception alters; our reactions are more measured; and our attitude becomes enlightened.

Step 1: Follow the basic procedures until you are seated comfortably and focussed inward.

Step 2: Picture yourself surrounded by a whole aura of golden light. Visualise gleaming particles of brilliant light dancing about you, sparkling like the sunbeams.

Let this golden light envelop you. Let it enter your eyes; let it enter deep into your heart and soul. Let your 'inside' be filled with the brilliant particles of golden light. Take the light in through your eyes, into your consciousness; shut your eyes and feel your inner self 'light up' brilliantly.

Breathe, in deeply, inhaling the 'golden' air around you. Let it permeate every pore of your body. Simultaneously, breathe out your negativity, frustration and 'woundedness'.

Take in the golden light until you feel it glowing within you, like a bright flame. Take it in, until you feel that *you* are beginning to glow.

Feel that you are truly 'enlightened' now – literally and metaphorically. Become aware that dark tendencies have now been driven out by the light within you.

Allow yourself to become open, tolerant and non-judgemental. Feel yourself ready to face unpleasant situations without getting hurt, angry, without retreating from those you love. Dismiss the idea that you are a victim. Let the light within you emanate to the world outside, filling your entire world with light.

Step 3: As you come out of the meditation, breathe out love and understanding to the people you love, the people you work with, even those who have hurt you. As you breathe in, inhale the golden light of love and understanding.

5) Meditation On Recovery And Healing After The Loss Of A Loved One

In the Hindu way of life, death is not the closure or an ending. It is but an entry into another state of being, beyond the physical one with which we are all familiar.

Many spiritual traditions look upon death as a great teacher, a stern but essential preceptor. We are told that Tibetan Buddhist novices are actually sent out to meditate in graveyards so that they might learn to face up to the fact of their own mortality – and learn that life is precious. When we realise that death is inevitable, that it must come to all of us sooner or later, we will learn to be grateful for life, and we will learn to appreciate our near and dear ones more – for who knows when they will be taken away from us?

All of us experience bereavement and mourning at one stage or another in our lives. Hindu *samskaras* (rituals) make the family members go through a systematic, sometimes extended process of mourning – which itself becomes part of the healing process. But then, as Dr. Rachel Harris points out, healing occurs at a different level of being than mourning; because it involves a transformation of each one of us as a whole person. She adds, "It is important to recognise that healing is a larger process than mourning."

The death of a loved one leaves us empty, numb, emotionally paralysed. We cry our hearts out; we lean upon friends and family for support; but the empty space in our life and our hearts still continues to hurt us.

People will vouch for the fact that the death of a loved one can challenge our faith more than any other experience in life. One is not merely bereaved; one becomes bitter; one blames God; one begins to assume that He is unfair.

The pain needs to be eased; the hurt needs to be healed; the loss needs to be accepted and dealt with at the physical, emotional and spiritual level. It is not enough for us to survive the loss – but to grow stronger and braver and more "whole" so that we may learn to sustain and support those who need us and our love. We need to go through a process of healing that can truly transform us.

Step 1: Follow the basic procedures until you are seated comfortably and focussed inward.

Step 2: Visualise yourself seated before your *ishta devta* (chosen deity). Allow yourself to feel the anger, hurt and resentment you hold against Him. Feel them fully and think of how best you can express them.

Seek God's permission to express your anger. Visualise Him telling you, "Go ahead and tell Me whatever you feel about Me. Go ahead and express the full range of your feelings against Me. I am ready to hear your feelings and accept them, too."

Take your time to tell God why you feel hurt, let down and betrayed. Just go ahead and deliver a non-verbal mental monologue to Him, not sparing the least detail.

When you feel you are through, allow yourself to explore your own anger and loss. Do not blame yourself or criticise yourself for your inadequacy or short comings. Your anger and bitterness are a legitimate part of your relationship with God; they are part of the process of your spiritual unfolding.

When this exercise is repeated over a period of time, you will find not only your anger lessens in intensity, but you will actually find that you are seeking guidance. Once your anger has been displaced, other feelings and insights will emerge spontaneously. Your faith is reborn, renewed, revitalised.

Step 3: As you breathe in, feel that your spirit is unfolding. As you breathe out tell yourself that you trust the world, that you trust life and that your faith in God will carry you through your darkest days.

6) Communing With Your Loved Ones Beyond Life

Sometimes, death steals upon people unannounced, unexpected, and, obviously, unwanted. One minute, we are making plans for tomorrow, plans for next week, plans for the future, plans for a wedding or a family event – and then, the bottom seems to drop out from life. Our loved ones are snatched away without warning.

The unspoken words, unexpressed sentiments, the whole 'unfinished transactions' with our loved ones who are no more, can be a heavy burden to bear for even the strongest among us. We may have hurt them, and now we cannot apologise or, it may be that *they* have hurt us, and our anger and resentment are now futile.

As I said, the Hindu system of philosophy teaches us that death is simply another state of being. As the sun sets in one continent, it is rising in another; so too, death upon this earth plane, is a birth into another. If we wish to commune with our loved ones, we can reach out to them through repeated exercise of this particular meditation.

Step 1: Follow the basic procedures until you are seated comfortably and focussed inward.

Step 2: Dwell on the memories of your loved one. Evoke a picture of him/her in your mental vision. Recall the much loved form and face; remember the well loved voice; recreate the warmth of the touch, the reassuring smell of being close to the loved one.

Now, begin to 're-play' mentally, the experiences that happened to you with this person: include the happy and unhappy events, the joys and sorrows you shared, the quarrels and misunderstandings that you went through.

When the 're-play' is over, wait for the communication to begin. Sometimes, it may be just one-sided – from you, or from the other person. Sometimes, it may be a two-way utterance; it may be in silence, or it may be in unspoken words. Allow the communication to take place. This is your opportunity to complete 'unfinished transactions', and you can return to this process whenever you need.

Step 3: As you breathe in, inhale acceptance, understanding and peace. As you breathe out, exhale a loving farewell to the dear departed one for now. Experience peace and stillness descending on you.

Repeat this exercise over a period of months until you feel at peace within, and feel, too, that your unfinished transactions have now been completed.

7) Meditation On Coping With Stress And Tension At Work

My faith in God and Guru has made me an eternal optimist. I strongly believe with Browning that "God's in His Heaven, and all's right with the world." I assert again and again to my friends: "All was well, all is well, and all shall be well, tomorrow, and a thousand years hence."

While I celebrate the positive approach to life, I will be the last person to deny that there is a negative side to life. Life can throw up difficult situations, put difficult people on our path: we find ourselves in high-stress situations, unable to cope. We need to retain our inner sense of balance; we need the confidence to handle the problem successfully; we need to be sure that we can rise to the occasion!

Step 1: Follow the basic procedures until you are seated comfortably and focussed inward.

Step 2: Picture yourself standing on the sea shore. Before you, the vast, deep blue ocean stretches endlessly. On the shore is a sturdy, rowing boat, ready to go out to sea.

Scattered at your feet are numerous sea-shells, sea-weeds and other flotsam and jetsam that you normally find on beaches. These, in fact, are symbolic of the 'mess' your life is in, due to the unsolvable problem you are dealing with.

Visualise yourself beginning to work systematically. Gather the debris all around you and put them together in a carton, container or box that has been left on the beach for you, for this purpose. Working patiently and quietly, clean up, clear up the small stretch of beach that you are standing on. Pile all the stuff into the carton and put it on the boat.

Now picture yourself rowing out into the sea in the boat. (This is a beautiful fantasy, so you can take it for granted that you are an excellent oarsman.) Row out into the sea and enjoy the brilliance of blue waters all around you, and the vast blue canvas of the sky above. When you have rowed enough, dump the contents of the carton – seaweeds, seashells, flotsam and jetsam – and watch them float, sink, disappear into the depths. Make sure the carton is absolutely empty.

Now, row back to the beach, enjoying a sense of freedom and peace. Your 'problem' is non-existent.

Step 3: As you breathe in, feel a sense of peace and calm. As you breathe out, feel a new courage and confidence in yourself and the world around you.

8) Cultivating Peace

Peace and happiness go hand in hand. What we imagine to be 'happiness' is often nothing but a momentary, transitory feeling of pleasure. True joy is closely allied to peace. I give you Sharon Selzberg's definition of joy and peace:

> Alas, for many of us, such moments of peace are too fleeting; if we wish to experience this peace, calm and stillness *within* us, irrespective of what is happening in our lives, we need to cultivate an inner core, an inner centre of peace – deep within us, a centre of peace to which we can retreat whenever we wish, that nothing can disturb and nothing can dispel.

This exercise is so simple and so easy, that you can practise it daily, in sessions of 5 – 10 minute session.

Step 1: Follow the basic procedures until you are seated comfortably and focussed inward.

Step 2: Now imagine that as you breathe in, you are inhaling the peace of God, the peace that passeth, surpasseth understanding. As you breathe out, you are exhaling calmness all around. There is peace within you, there is calm all around you. Reflect on this beautiful passage from the Vedas:

> May there be peace in the higher regions; may there be peace in the firmament; may the waters flow peacefully; may all the divine powers bring unto us peace. The Supreme Lord is Peace. May we all dwell in peace, peace, peace; and may that peace come into each of us.

Step 3: During the last two minutes of this exercise, become aware of the rhythm of your breathing. Open your eyes gently and feel peace infusing your body, mind, heart and soul.

I would request you, in your own interest, to try these meditation exercises, because they are simple and easy to follow. They can be practised anywhere, at anytime, with a minimum of fuss. All you need to do, as I have repeatedly said, is to be focussed inward.

These exercises really do not demand external 'facilities'. They are really 'inner' activities, or 'spiritual retreats'. After all your inner life, your inner world is ever present within, like the unseen, unmapped River Saraswati at the *Triveni Sangamam* in the holy city of Allahabad, where the Ganga and the Yamuna merge visibly – while the undercurrent of the Saraswati is ever present, although never seen.

This inner world is also ever present within you, and you can 'connect' to it anytime you wish, to tap the healing, soothing, enlightening power of the superconscious.

Of course, a 'sacred space' is condusive to these exercises. Vast, ancient temples, high-vaulted, beautiful cathedrals, mosques, synagogues, monasteries, *satsang* halls, *ashramas* and the abodes of holy ones can all provide a beautiful retreat for you.

If you have visited such sacred spaces, remember your feelings when you entered these places; recreate the atmosphere in your heart; rekindle the sense of awe, mystery and wonder that you felt there; and you will find that you have created your own sacred space!

There is one important point that I wish to stress: as you come out of these spiritual exercises, make sure you carry the insights, awareness and calmness you have gained therefrom, into your workaday world. This is to ensure that these 'retreats' add a spiritual dimension to your daily life and enhance the spiritual quality of your life.

FAQs On The Ladder Of *Abhyasa*

What is true discipline?

True discipline is self-discipline. It was self-discipline that was inculcated in the *ashramas* of ancient India. The teacher — the *Guru* — was not a task-Master. He encouraged students to develop self-discipline. You see, the teacher is not always with us, but we are always with ourselves. If we are trained to be disciplined, we will always be disciplined.

Therefore, we were taught that there is One who is watching us all the time. God is watching us. God is watching over us. Today, all this is forgotten. Even if God is a hypothesis, as so many people today declare, He is a very helpful hypothesis. But, God is not a mere hypothesis, God is real. God is actual.

How can young people cultivate self-discipline?

When Benjamin Franklin was a boy, he divided his day and night into compartments of fifteen minutes each. Every hour had four compartments. He said to himself, "So many compartments, I will devote to sleep, so many compartments, I will give to looking after the body. So many compartments, I will give to games." He led a disciplined life as a boy. Benjamin Franklin did not waver from the programme he had fixed for himself. Our way may not be the way of Benjamin Franklin—that was just an example. But, we must live a life of discipline.

I think that discipline is lacking in our lives. Discipline is conspicuous by its absence. There is no discipline in the home. There is no discipline in the school. In the home, the girl turns thirteen and the parents dare not ask, "Where are you going?" I was in London and the parents said, "We want to set a curfew for our daughter." They said to her, "You have to come home by 11:30 p.m." She laughed, saying, "How can I come home before 11:30 p.m.? Our programmes commence at 11:30 p.m." The girl returned at 2:30 in the morning. She did not listen to her parents. There is no discipline.

In our days, we dared not come home a minute later than 8:30 in the night. For you, 8:30 is not even the beginning of having fun. We were not allowed to go to the movies. You may be surprised to know that until I did my post-graduation, I had seen just one movie: it was called Ben Hur. We were not allowed to touch playing cards. I don't even know how to shuffle a pack of playing cards. In those days, we had discipline in our families, in our schools, with our teachers. Today, teachers are afraid of their students. The whole world has become topsy-turvy. Values have gone mad.

What is freedom?

Freedom is not that you can do what you like. Freedom is to be able to do what you ought to do, what you should do.

How can we be alert and cultivate self-control and self-discipline?

This has to be a process. It can't be accomplished overnight or in a moment. In the *Upanishads*, the *rishis* tell us that at every step in the round of life, we are given a choice. Do we want to follow the path of *preya* (pleasant) or the path of *shreya* (good). The path of *preya* is a smooth, slippery path, but it can lead to our doom. The path of *shreya* is a stony and a thorny path, sometimes paved with flames, but it leads us to our good. We must grow in the path of self-discipline. This means that you have to make the right choice and stick to it whatever may be the conditions.

Dadaji, How does a beginner learn to meditate?

To meditate you must first learn to concentrate. Concentrate on one idea, one object, one Name. When you have grown in concentration, then meditation becomes very easy. I sit in the lotus posture; I close my eyes and try to meditate. But because I have not yet learnt concentration, my mind wavers. It keeps on drifting from one thought to another. So concentration is the first step on the path of meditation.

How can we grow in concentration?

The question has been answered in the *Bhagavad Gita*. Arjuna puts this question to the Master. "The mind is more restless than a storm. Will I be able to control it?" and Sri Krishna says, "It may not be easy to control the mind but it is possible. You can control the mind by these two means, *abhyasa* and *vairagya*."

Abhyasa is doing the same thing over and over again. We are slaves to our habits which have become a part of our nature. Now we have to form or reform new habits.

Vairagya is the spirit of detachment. You realise that all that you see, all that you touch, all that you conceive is passing, it has no value.

Can you suggest some practical exercise for concentration?

There is one very simple exercise in concentration. Let the candle flame be burning in front of you. Keep it at eye level and keep on looking at the candle flame. After a while, close your eyes and try to concentrate on the flame. You will see the candle flame burning in your mind's eye. Then gradually it will fade away. Again open your eyes and repeat the exercise. You could also do a similar exercise with a picture of your *ishta deva* – Sri Krishna, Mahadeva or Sri Rama, Jesus, Guru Nanak, Baha'u'llah, Buddha. Keep a picture at eye level, open your eyes, and concentrate on the Form. Then, close your eyes. You will see that Form for a little while, and then it will fade away. Keep on doing it. You will grow in concentration.

There is yet another exercise which is known as *tratak*. It is keeping your eyes fixed on a candle flame, but you must not blink. The eyes must be open all the time. Water will flow out of your eyes. It is as though you are weeping, shedding tears, but you should not close your eyes. As you do this, you will grow in concentration.

Concentration is the very foundation of meditation.

Can listening to instrumental music help in meditation?

It can. There is a type of meditation based on music. There are a number of *sufi* saints who tell us that music can take you to the seventh plane. But it should be music of the right type, music which should wake up the dormant spirit within you.

Sometimes we reach or achieve higher levels for short periods of time but fall down again. What should we do to sustain further?

I think what is needed is inner purification. If only you can purify yourself, all these experiences that make you feel that you have reached certain spiritual heights – all these experiences will become natural. You shouldn't strive to achieve certain experiences. All you need to strive for is inner purification. Purity is going to take you to that point. Blessed are the pure in heart for they shall see God. But the spiritual path is very much like a mountain climb. When you climb a mountain, you go up, but again, you have to pass through a valley to be able to rise still higher. So when you are in the valley, be not depressed. It is only a part of the path that will lead you to the highest.

If I sleep less, and I sit in meditation, I feel drowsy and even go to sleep and dream.

You must not sleep less but you must sleep well. Whatever work you do, you should do it well. When you meditate, you should meditate. When you sleep, you should sleep. When you get up from your sleep and find that you are drowsy, it only means that you need more sleep. You should not meditate when you are feeling drowsy, because then you will not be able to meditate, you will vegetate. When you sit to meditate, you must have a feeling of freshness.

Dada, can you offer us some guidelines for meditation?

Meditation is being regarded now by an ever increasing number of scientists, as a 20th and a 21st century medicine. Their research has shown that meditation alters the activity of the nervous system in such a way that a creative energy of the individual is recharged.

Success in meditation is closely related to peaceful living. For meditation to be fruitful, the mind must be calm, and for that it is necessary for man to conduct his normal life and activities in a peaceful, loving manner.

Following are the practical suggestions on how to meditate:

1. Sit in silence in an easy and comfortable posture with the spinal cord, the neck and head in a straight line.
2. Practise meditation preferably at the same place and at the same time, everyday.
3. Sit facing the east or the north.
4. Go to God as you are – with your sins and imperfections.
5. Think of an object or a symbol or an incident from the life of a great one.
6. As you sit in silence, wear a soft smile.
7. Let your daily life be one of sacrifice.

Is not meditation meant for those who have nothing to do with the workaday world?

The life of meditation is not the life of a hermit, which keeps us aloof from our fellow-men. Rather, through meditation, our sympathies are quickened, our perceptions grow keener, our feelings deepen, we grow in unselfishness and perform our duties with greater efficiency. Through meditation we contact a Source of tremendous power which is within each one of us but of which many of us are not aware.

I believe that a few minutes of meditation everyday is essential for peace of mind. However, I have a tough time clearing my mind of all thoughts and simply cannot focus on the Supreme Lord. How can I tackle this problem?

The mind has acquired this habit of wandering – not through this birth merely, but through birth after birth. Let me tell you the story of *Mullah* Nasruddin. He would sit everyday for eight hours, in silence, with his ear against the wall. He did this day after day.

One day, his wife asked him, "*Mullah* you sit with your ear stuck to the wall everyday. Tell me, what do you hear?

The *Mullah* replied, "If you wish to hear what I hear, you must come and sit here yourself." Next morning, the wife got up very early and prepared the day's meals quickly, so that she would be free to go and sit all day with her ear against the wall. She sat for four long hours– but she heard nothing.

Exasperated, she said to the *Mullah*, "I have sat here for four hours and I have heard nothing. I am tired and I am giving up now."

The *Mullah* retorted, "You want to give up after four hours. I have been sitting thus for eight hours everyday for the last 28 years, I have not heard anything either. But I do not give up!"

It is this persistence that you need when you sit in silence!

There is a simple breathing exercise suggested by the Vietnamese Buddhist Master, Thich Nhat Hanh, which may help you to grow in concentration.

1) Close your eyes. Become aware of the breathing process – the going in and coming out of your breath.

2) As you breathe in, say to yourself, "I am aware that the breath is going in." As you breathe out, say to yourself, "I am aware that the breath is coming out." Repeat this five times saying "in" and "out".

3) As you inhale, say to yourself, "I am aware that the breath is becoming deep." As you exhale, say to yourself, "I am aware that my breath is becoming slow." Do this five times repeating, "D-e-e-p", as you inhale, "s-l-o-w" as you exhale.

4) At the next step, say to yourself as you inhale, "I am aware of the present moment as I breathe in." when you exhale, say to yourself, "I know that this moment is perfect." Do this five times repeating "P-r-e-s-e-n-t" as you breathe in; "P-e-r-f-e-c-t" as you breathe out.

5) Repeat the word "c-a-l-m" as you inhale; repeat the word "r-e-l-a-x" as you exhale, five times.

This exercise in breathing will help you considerably with your meditation.

Breathing is with you 24 hours a day – you are never without it, it is your best friend. Use it to harness the power of concentration.

Can you tell us about the type of meditation preached and practised by the Buddha?

The Buddha speaks of five types of meditation. The first is the meditation of love in which we so adjust our heart that we wish for the happiness of all living things, including the happiness of our enemies.

The second is the meditation of compassion, in which we think of all beings in distress, vividly representing in our imagination their sorrows and anxieties so as to arouse a deep compassion for them within us.

The third is the meditation of joy in which we think of the prosperity of others and rejoice with their rejoicings.

The fourth is the meditation on impurity, in which we think of the evil consequences of immorality and corruption. In this meditation, we realise how trivial is the pleasure of the moment and how fatal are its consequences!

The fifth is the meditation of serenity, in which we rise above love and hate, tyranny and wealth and want, and regard our own fate with impartial calm and perfect tranquillity.

What is the most valuable asset God has given us?

More precious than gold and silver, greater than the greatest wealth, greater than any asset, is the mind. In your mind, you have a 24-hour friend. You may be alone, helpless or in distress, but your mind is ever ready to help you and to guide you to overcome any situation. It is your precious friend, an invaluable asset. Only use it in the right way. Do not let the mind be your Master. Let it be a fellow-servant in the service of God and suffering humanity.

How do we train our minds?

Thoughts have power. So let us be careful of our thoughts and utilise all the power available to us in the service of suffering humanity. The brain has been called a "fabulous mechanism". It is about the size of half a grape-fruit but it is truly a most wonderful thing. It is capable of recording eight hundred memories per second for seventy five years without exhausting itself. It is a storehouse of between ten billion and one hundred billion pieces of information. Even the most powerful computers in the world have memories that hold only a few million items of accessible information. The human brain retains everything that it takes in and never forgets anything. Even though we don't recall all the information received, everything is on a permanent file in our brain.

If a computer were to be built to match the brain's potential, it would occupy space comparable to the size of one of the tallest buildings in the world – the Empire State Building – and need one billion watts of electrical power to run. The cost would work out to an astronomical figure.

The mind is one of God's amazing gifts to man. Scientists tell us that we use only one-fiftieth of the brain power available to us. Let us train our minds and ourselves to use this fabulous power in the right way. Therefore, let us take care of our thoughts.

What exactly is intuition or sixth sense as we call it?

Intuition is the gift of knowing things which the mind does not know or understand. Our knowledge is based on what the senses tell us and what the mind decides. But that may not be the whole truth. The senses very often betray us. The mind often jumps to wrong conclusions. Then it is that intuition takes over. Intuition knows, intuition understands. It is here that women excel men. Men have tuition but they don't have intuition. They have sight but they don't have insight.

You have spoken of shampooing our mind everyday. I would like to ask you to give us a few practical ways of doing this.

Shampooing means cleansing. Now, we need to cleanse our minds, we need to unclutter our minds. Our minds are full of wrong thinking, wrong ideas. The minds of so many of us are negative. We must cleanse them of their negativity. To do this, we must get right down into our consciousness and cleanse ourselves of all those rotten thoughts that hold us captive today – thoughts of impurity, selfishness, greed, lust and hatred.

There are so many who nurture in their minds, thoughts of hatred against others. I remember when I was a school boy, there was a classmate of mine, who started hating me, I don't know why. One night, as I was moving in the street, he took a big stick and aimed it at me. If it had hit me, my legs would have been broken. I was only 11 to 12 years old then. But I did not hate him in return. I went and embraced him and said to him, "What is your difficulty? Have I hurt you? Have I done any harm to you?" Then he said, "I find that you are allowed to enter the house of the girl who I love and they don't allow me to enter." I told him, "That is not my fault. If you wish, from today I will not go there, I am not interested in her." Then he understood me and hatred turned into friendship.

Our minds should be clean and uncluttered. It is only then that we can hope to be happy. Otherwise, with all those dirty thoughts in the mind within, how can we be at peace with ourselves? Whenever I used to get

193

unwanted thoughts, even though I was sitting in the classroom and the teacher was lecturing, I would immediately slap myself. My classmate sitting near me would ask me what the matter was. I would say it was a mosquito. But it was an internal mosquito, not an external one. Therefore, whenever you find a negative or an undesirable thought waking up in the mind within you, slap yourself immediately.

Sadhu Vaswani, as a young boy, used to keep a pin with himself. Whenever he found an undesirable thought waking up within him, he would just pierce the pin into his flesh until the body felt so much pain that the mind would cry out, "Forgive me, forgive me! I will not think such a thought again."

What is the difference between soul and mind?

The mind is an instrument of cognition, of knowing things, knowing the material world. The soul is the ray of God, that which you essentially are. The mind is an instrument with which we know. We try to understand things. The soul is immortal, the mind is mortal. The mind is discursive, the soul is synergic. The soul integrates everything but the mind analyses.

We need the help of the mind in doing the work on the physical plane. That is why we have brought with ourselves the instrument of the mind. Out of God emanate many rays, every ray is a soul. This is what makes all of us one. The soul is universal. The mind is individual. The mind individualises but the soul unites.

How can we quieten the mind?

The easiest way is to engage in a loving and intimate conversation with God. There is another way in which you go over all things that you have done in the past 24 hours, in the reverse order until you get to the first hour. You will see that there are many things that you should not have done, but which you did, as there are many things you should have done, but which you did not do. They are known as the acts of omission and commission. Ask God's forgiveness and for the strength and wisdom not to repeat such acts in future.

How may we cultivate the subconscious mind?

1. Always entertain positive thoughts. Never harbour thoughts of jealousy, hatred or lust.
2. Do not react emotionally to things that happen.
3. Never make any negative suggestions in regard to what you want to be. Thus, for instance, never say, I have a bad memory. This will only lead to loss of memory. Rather say my memory is improving.
4. Never hate or resent people. Let love and forgiveness be the law of your life. Many types of illnesses are caused by intense hatred and resentment.
5. Read books that inspire and uplift you rather than books that feature violence, sex, crime and other acts of viciousness. This is specially important in the case of children and youth.

Is inward beauty a matter of the mind?

Inward beauty, I believe, is the beauty of thoughts, aspirations and prayers. If our thoughts are pure, if our aspirations are pure and beautiful, and desires likewise pure and beautiful, we are beautiful within.

Each one of us gets impure thoughts again and again. Dirty emotions wake up within us. We are sitting at a holy place. Suddenly seemingly out of nowhere, an evil desire wakes up within us. An evil thought comes to

195

us. If we let that thought or emotion stay with us, it will be like a stain on our interior life. It is a blot.

Socrates used to pray again and again, "God, make me beautiful within!" If you desire, if you are eager, if you wish to grow beautiful within, then you must build your life in purity. This is very essential. Every impure impulse, impure thought, impure emotion that wakes up within us, spoils our interior beauty. Therefore, the second step is prayer. Keep on praying again and again if you want to grow beautiful within.

All these years, we have been wandering with the mind, doing nothing, gathering nothing. Instead of letting the mind wander after useless things, pick up a great thought – of a great one. It may be a *sloka* from the *Bhagavad Gita* or a line from the *Sant Bani* or the *Gurbani*. Let us keep on repeating the great thought and try to enter into the depths of the meanings of the words we repeat. This will help considerably in controlling the wandering of the mind.

What is Silence?

Silence, is two-fold. There is outer silence: it is absence of noise, freedom from the shouts and tumults of daily life. And there is interior silence: it is freedom from the clamour of desires, cessation of mental acrobatics, stilling of the play of conflicting forces. It is the peace that passeth, surpasseth understanding. The seers of ancient India called it "*turiya*", which means the "fourth". It is the fourth stage. May you and I aspire to reach this stage! Not until we have reached it, can we hope to experience unbroken joy and peace and harmony for which our distracted hearts have been crying.

You often speak of silence as an appointment with God. How can we cultivate this silence in this age of technology, where we are surrounded by sounds and activity?

It is a fact that the great need of man is silence. To help us to avoid stress and tension, the noted psychologist, Deborah Bright, recommends twenty minutes of PQT twice a day. PQT stands for personal quiet time.

Even as particles of dust cling to our clothes, so too, particles of noise cling to our hearts. To clean our clothes, we wash them with soap and water. Even so, to cleanse our souls, we need to take a dip in the waters of silence. Thus, it is necessary to practise silence every day.

Why is silence said to be golden? Is not speech a great gift given to us?

Let silence be the law of your life: for silence hurts no one. When you feel like breaking your silence, ask yourself if what you have to say is something better than silence. If so, say it; else remain silent.

If only we could collect the words each one of us speaks, what a huge mountain they would make! Himalayas of words have passed through these tiny lips. All these words come under five categories:

1. Words inspired by love of God. These are the words we utter in adoration of the Eternal – the cry of the soul to the Over Soul, the songs sung in praise of the Most High, prayer, *kirtan* and *japa* of the sacred Name.
2. Words inspired by love of fellow-men. These are the words of comfort and consolation we pass on to

those who suffer and struggle and are in sorrow –
words which cheer them on life's lonesome way.

3. Words which wound and hurt and kill. These are
the words inspired by jealousy, envy, anger, malice
or hatred. How often do we not speak ill of others,
little knowing what havoc we cause! An archer
shoots to kill. More dangerous is the man with a
forked tongue. Every time he opens his lips, he sends
forth shafts which strike and sting.

4. Words inspired by self-love. These are the words
prompted by egoism, by greed and sensuality. How
often do we not brag about our so-called
achievements or speak in self-righteous pride! And
see, how happy men feel when they indulge in
obscene and sensual talk! When it comes to making
a little material gain, men, alas, have no hesitation
in speaking an untruth. They gain a little and lose
their all.

5. Idle words. These are the words men utter without
rhyme or reason, merely to while away their time.
The conversations of men are filled with silly
questions and imbecile answers, which make our
homes centres of idle gossip and our clubs and
meeting-places so many 'Towers of Babel'. Against
this type of talk did Jesus warn, when he said, "But
I say unto you, that for every idle word that men
speak, they shall have to render account, on the day
of judgement." This saying is not given us in the
Gospels, but in one of the Eastern accounts of Jesus.

When you purchase an earthen vessel, you strike it,
and from the sound, make out if it is cracked or not. So,
too, is the integrity of man proved by his speech. If the
words a man utters belong to the first two classes, verily

198

is he blessed among mortals. Such a one spreads sunshine wherever he goes!

Is it true that silence can give us insight into our lives and tell us where we come from, what we are doing and where we will go from here?

As you enter into silence, you will realise this truth – that you are from the Kingdom of God, that you are going to the Kingdom of God, and that this Kingdom of God is not apart from you, it is right within you!

Our journey is an interior journey. It is the journey in consciousness. Today, we find that for many of us, our consciousness is imprisoned in what we call the lower *chakras*. Silence can be a process by which we may free our consciousness from low feelings, raising it step by step, we may arrive at the Kingdom of God within us. We don't have to ascend the skies to reach heaven. It is right here, within us.

All spiritual teachers tell us that we are dwellers in the dark. What is the way of coming out of the darkness that envelops us?

It is the way of turning within! Alas, we are busy with many things, but have neglected the one thing needful. We keep chasing shadow-shapes which come and go. When shall we learn to turn within?

Man came to the earth as a pilgrim, but has become a wanderer. Even in our spiritual quest, we wander from creed to creed, from one school or thought to another, and are filled with unrest. We move to temples and churches and places of pilgrimage—and meet with disappointment. For, not until we turn within, will we find that which we are seeking.

Truth is within! Wisdom is within! The Source of all strength is within! Therefore, turn within!

A beginning has to be made somewhere. Everyday, preferably at the same time and at the same place, let us sit in silence and pray, meditate, do our spiritual thinking. It is our daily appointment with God. We keep a number of appointments, everyday. Alas! We neglect this most important of all appointments – our daily appointment with God. He is not far away from us. He is wherever we are. He is here: He is now! All we have to do is to close our eyes, shut out the world and call Him – and there He is in front of us. In the beginning we may not see Him: let us be sure, that He sees us. We may not be able to immediately hear His Voice: but He hears us. The tiniest whisper of the human heart, the smallest stirring of the soul is audible to His ever-attentive ears. Speak to Him: open out your heart to Him: place all your difficulties before Him: and you will find wonderful things happen to you.

Glimpses of books by Dada J.P. Vaswani

Daily Inspiration: A Thought
for Every day of the Year
J P Vaswani
ISBN ...2157 8   Rs. 100

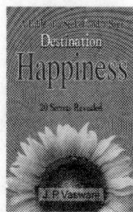

Destination Happiness
J.P. Vaswani
ISBN 81 207 3146 2
Rs. 250

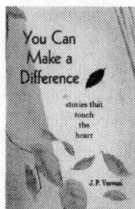

You Can Make a Difference
J.P. Vaswani
ISBN 81 207 3153 0
Rs. 100

It's All a Matter of Attitude!
J.P. Vaswani
ISBN 81 207 3150 6
Rs. 100

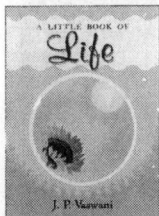

A Little Book of Life
J.P. Vaswani
ISBN 81 207 2581 6
Rs. 50

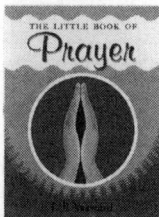

The Little Book of Prayer
J.P. Vaswani
ISBN 81 207 2582 4
Rs. 50

The Little Book of Service
J.P. Vaswani
ISBN 81 207 2584 0
Rs. 50

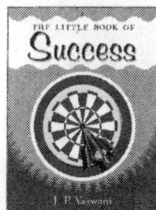

The Little Book of Success
J.P. Vaswani
ISBN 81 207 2585 9
Rs. 50

The Little Book of Freedom
from Stress
J.P. Vaswani
ISBN 81 207 2580 8
Rs. 50

A Little Book of Wisdom
J.P. Vaswani
ISBN 81 207 2587 5
Rs. 50

Swallow Irritation before
Irritation Swallows you
J.P. Vaswani
ISBN 81 207 3152 2
Rs. 125

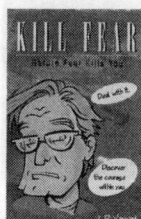

Kill Fear before Fear Kills You
J.P. Vaswani
ISBN 81 207 3151 4
Rs. 100

The Magic of Forgiveness
J P Vaswani
ISBN ...2900 5   Rs. 90

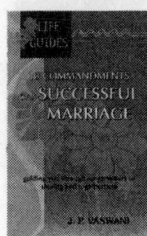

10 Commandments of a
Successful Marriage
J P Vaswani
ISBN ...2897 1   Rs. 90

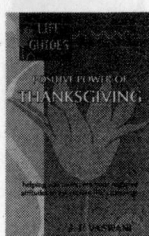

Positive Power of
Thanksgiving
J P Vaswani
ISBN ...2899 8   Rs. 90

Secrets of Health &
Happiness
J P Vaswani
ISBN ...2898 X   Rs. 90

Moments with a Master
Sandhya S Nankani
ISBN ...2459 3 Rs. 150

Dada J.P. Vaswani: His Life &
Teachings
*Krishna Kumari & Prabha
Sampath*
ISBN ...2461 5   Rs. 300

Sadhu Vaswani: His Life &
Teachings
J P Vaswani
ISBN ...2462 3   Rs. 250

The Seven Commandments of
the Bhagavad Gita
J.P. Vaswani
ISBN 81 207 3145 X
Rs. 250

Dost Thou Keep Memory?
*Puja Lalmalani &
Sandhya Nankani*
ISBN ...2704 5 Rs. 225

What You Would Like to
Know about Hinduism
J P Vaswani
ISBN ...2583 2   Rs. 95

ईश्वर तुझे प्रणाम
ISBN 81 207 3135 2
Rs. 100

आत्मिक जलपान
(जनवरी-जून)
जे पी वासवानी
ISBN ...2478 X   Rs. 100

प्रार्थना की शक्ति
ISBN 81 207 3136 0
Rs. 50

संतों की लीला
जे पी वासवानी
ISBN ...2773 8   Rs. 75

साधु वासवानी उनका
जीवन और शिक्षाएं
जे पी वासवानी
ISBN ...2902 1 Rs. 200

भक्तों की उलझनों का
सरल उपाय
जे पी वासवानी
ISBN ...2901 3   Rs. 75

दैनिक प्रेरणा: वर्ष के प्रत्येक
दिन के लिये एक विचार
जे पी वासवानी
ISBN ...2458 5   Rs. 75

आत्मिक पोषण
(जुलाई-दिसम्बर)
जे पी वासवानी
ISBN ...2535 2   Rs. 100

अलवर संतों की महान
गाथायें
जे पी वासवानी
ISBN ...2769 X   Rs. 75

Nuri Granth
Sadhu T L Vaswani
ISBN ...2590 5 Rs. 500